Patterns in Jewish History: Insights into the Past, Present and Future of the Eternal People

מגיד
MAGGID

Other works by the author

Vision and Valor

The Oral Law of Sinai

Tending the Vineyard

Living Jewish

Sand and Stars
[*by Yaffa Ganz in collaboration with Berel Wein*]

Echoes of Glory

Herald of Destiny

Triumph of Survival

Faith and Fate

Buy Green Bananas

Second Thoughts

The Pesach Haggadah

Pirkei Avos

In Hebrew

Ḥikrei Halakha

Iyunim BeMassekhtot HaTalmud [*two volumes*]

Ḥukkei Ḥayyim: Saviv Yeraḥ HaEitanim

Rabbi Berel Wein

PATTERNS in JEWISH HISTORY

Insights into the Past, Present & Future of the Eternal People

Maggid Books

Patterns in Jewish History: Insights into the Past, Present and Future of the Eternal People

First Edition, 2011
Maggid Books
An imprint of Koren Publishers Jerusalem Ltd.

POB 8531, New Milford, CT 06776-8531, USA
POB 2455, London W1A 5WY, England
& POB 4044, Jerusalem 91040, Israel

www.korenpub.com

ISBN 978 159 264 326 4, *hardcover*

A CIP catalogue record for this title is available from the British Library

Printed in USA

To Mira

Contents

Acknowledgements

My interest in Jewish history goes back sixty years to when I was a fledgling student at Yeshivat Beit HaMidrash LaTorah (Hebrew Theological College) in Chicago, Illinois. The college is currently located in Skokie, Illinois, a suburb of Chicago. During my student years, the provided lunches being less than sumptuous, I found myself in the library for many a lunch hour. The librarian, Mrs. Leah Mishkin *z"l*, whetted my appetite – not for lunch – but for books on Jewish history and biography. Later I studied Jewish history at the college under Professors Meyer Waxman, Leonard Mishkin and Eliezer Berkovits. My Talmud teachers also taught me Jewish history, though only indirectly, by imparting to me the values and traditions of the ages as reflected in the Torah and the Talmud and the later rabbinic writings. They may not have taught me the exact facts and dates that form much of the academic study of history, but they provided the insights, vignettes and nuances that made the subject come alive for me. All of my life I have been hooked on knowing as much as I could about my people and, through this, about myself as well. My parents encouraged me in this matter and did not allow me to fall into the trap of believing that this knowledge was impractical and unnecessary.

When I was a congregational rabbi in Miami Beach I began to deliver regular courses and lectures in Jewish history to the women's groups of the synagogue. The men apparently felt that the subject was not worthy of their time. Later in my rabbinic career when I moved to Suffern, New York, I continued my history classes for the women of the community. Eventually a cadre of men, urged on by their wives' erudition and their own ignorance of Jewish history, asked me to conduct a series of lectures for them one night a week. A number of these students were physicians who naturally found it difficult to attend the classes on a consistent and regular basis. So the idea of recording the lectures on audiotapes was born. I then headed Yeshiva Shaarei Torah in Suffern, New York and taught history there as well. The sale of my recorded audiotapes blossomed into a major source of income for the yeshiva. As I was then already planning to immigrate to Israel, I set up the Destiny Foundation to disseminate all of the materials regarding Jewish history that I was producing. Now offering audio recordings, CDs, DVDs, MP3s, YouTube snippets, lectures and books, it has become a major educational resource in the world of Jewish education today.

I had written three works of Talmudic analysis and commentary that were published here in Israel. I was working on a fourth volume when I met a man walking on the street here in Jerusalem. I had no idea who he was but he approached me and said, "There are many others that are writing books on Talmudic subjects. You should be writing on Jewish history!" And then he disappeared into the crowd. I took his words seriously – who knows who sent him to me? – and I then began writing about Jewish history. This is my seventh book on the subject.

I am gratified to have Koren Publishers Jerusalem publish this book under their Maggid imprint. Matthew Miller has been a true friend and Rachel Meghnagi has been a great editor. My wife, children and grandchildren have helped me enormously with their encouragement and support for the creation of this book and for all of my projects. Elaine Gilbert, The Cubac family and the entire staff of the Destiny Foundation, both here in Jerusalem and in Monsey, New York, have been my loyal and talented helpers for many years. The Destiny Foundation could not have existed all this time but for them.

I have done a great deal of research for this work. Nevertheless, humans, even rabbis, are prone to errors. I am solely responsible for the contents of this volume and pray that it be acceptable to its readers and even inspirational to coming generations over the years.

Preface

One of the basic questions always asked about history generally and Jewish history particularly is: "Does history always repeat itself?" The great Jewish answer to this question, delivered with the uniquely Jewish shrug of one's shoulders, is: "Maybe, it all depends." Unlike Marxism and other fatalistic predetermined ideas of the human story, which are subject to iron and immutable processes of economics, social classes, technological achievements and political systems, Judaism and Jewish life denies such rigid boundaries for human behavior. Judaism by its intrinsic nature and soaring belief is optimistic regarding the future of Israel and the world generally. The words of the great prophets of Israel regarding the almost utopian possibilities that the "latter days" will usher into human life, form the basis for this optimistic view of Judaism and Jews. We sincerely believe that a better tomorrow for all is possible, achievable and necessary. Yet Judaism points out to us the pitfalls that dot this road to a better world. It insists that we learn the lessons of the errors of the past, both the distant and the near past, in order to avoid foolishly repeating them. As the famous phrase goes, "Ignoring the mistakes of the past dooms us to repeat them." Or perhaps better still, "Insanity is repeating the same failed process over and over again."

Thus history is never to be ignored or demeaned. Even a cursory view of Jewish history will reveal definite patterns that rise and fall regularly in the story of the Eternal People. The purpose of this book is to trace and explain these patterns and thereby hopefully cast a light on our current and future state of being.

There are many basic questions that exist regarding the story of the Jewish people over the ages. How has this small people survived over the turbulent millennia of its existence? What are we to make of its vastly disproportionate influence and achievements vis-à-vis the societies of the human race generally? Why are there so few Jews, relatively speaking, in the world? Why is there so much hate and discrimination visited upon the Jewish people and, in our current world, the Jewish state of Israel? Why are there constantly so many divisions within the Jewish people which oftentimes result in the extreme hate and violence of Jew versus Jew? Is Judaism a religion, or a nation, or a family or what? And who is a Jew? These basic questions really trouble Jews and non-Jews and yet, over the centuries, satisfactory permanent answers to them have not received wide endorsement. Thus it is possible to trace, in the innumerable differing responses to these questions, patterns that exist in Jewish history and these patterns renew themselves on a fairly regular scale. The Jewish phrase was, and is, that understanding the problem is already half of its solution. In today's world, true understanding of the problems that face us is a rare commodity. We look at things very superficially with thirty-second sound bites that attempt to simplify complexities that have challenged us over the ages. I find in my life that simply knowing the complexities and difficulties that have faced my ancestors has been and is a strange sort of comfort to me. Realizing that I am not the first rabbi that has been accused simultaneously of being both too lenient and too strict (often at the very same moment in time), the first husband that does not always understand what is bugging his wife, and/or the first father of teenagers who is hopelessly out of touch, enables me to deal with these serious ego-destroying issues. There are clear patterns in private human life, just as there are in general Jewish history.

There was a time when the problems of life, and Jewish life particularly, were discussed and dealt with, inefficiently perhaps, but generally effectively, in the home and family. Judaism was always identified with having and supporting close family bonds, with all of the joys and pain that this entails. Children learned about life and gender, intimacy and domestic relations, the Jewish past and future, beliefs and mores and Jewish values all in their home and society. Schools did not occupy the place of honor and primacy that they now do in Jewish society. Though there were always books and scrolls present, true Jewish education was almost always taught on an individual basis, parent to child, tutor to pupil. In the chapter on Torah Study in this work, I hope to show how patterns in Jewish education arose, adapted, changed and reemerged again centuries later, albeit in a somewhat mutated form. Understanding how this previous situation differs from our present systems of transmitting our traditions and values will, I think, help illuminate the background to many of the problems, social, marital, family, communal and religious, that currently plague our society. The past can never be recaptured but it is always valuable to be aware of it and its instructional experiences. There is a tendency in Jewish life to actually change the past so that we will be more comfortable with it in the present and so that it will somehow now fit nicely into our preconceptions and current political and social correctness. By so doing one forfeits any chance of benefiting from that past. Only by seeing the pattern that emerges from the past and the present when viewed together can one have a sense of where current society stands and where it is headed, and how steps can be taken to improve its current lot and guarantee its future development.

Another phrase that has much popularity in human experience is "that the more things change the more they remain the same." Again the Jewish response is a shrug of the shoulders and a resounding maybe. Yet it is obvious to all students of history that human nature basically has not changed from the beginning of time till today. Humans' capacity for good or evil, honesty or mendacity, brutality or compassion, faith or rebellion, remains as unlimited and unchanged as it was upon Adam and Eve's expulsion from the Garden of Eden. But life circumstances certainly do change with the times and one would have to be blind and consummately ignorant not to realize that life in the twenty-first century in the West and Israel is far different than it was in seventeenth-century Poland or Iraq. Seeing the patterns of Jewish adaptation to new countries and climes, to new technology and discoveries, to differing social systems and political and governmental entities can help inform us as to the methods one can employ in dealing with our rapidly changing outside environment. Thus the Torah and its halakhic processes, which address the human condition head on without subterfuge and whitewash, remain unchangeable. But the methods and societies that it must deal with are not constant or static and therefore a recognition of the different patterns that have emerged in Jewish life over the ages regarding these ever challenging changes in society, education, social and political life and emerging value systems can only increase the greatness and growth of Torah and adorn it with larger glory.

In all candor, I bring no sense of omniscience to this project. I have studied Jewish history and written about it for many decades of my life. The Lord has blessed me that I have lived long enough to experience Jewish life over a number of differing generations, locations and circumstances. The Talmud teaches us that even when great wisdom may be lacking, age and experience still count for quite a bit. In my own years I have seen different patterns from the past reemerge in Jewish life, while certain ideas and general values that were sacrosanct in my youth have ebbed if not even disappeared. But the Torah that my father taught me as a child and young man has sustained me and all of Israel through a very dark and enormously complicated and challenging period of Jewish history.

All books written by authors are personal to the author himself. There is always a large piece of the author embedded in one's work no matter how factual and objective the presentation of the book may be. This book is a product of a number of lectures that I have delivered over the years to varying audiences. A number of people (not in overwhelming numbers, but quality always trumps quantity) have spurred me to develop this idea of patterns in Jewish history into a book. My friend, Shmuel Blitz, provided the necessary encouragement for me to undertake this venture. Writing this book has enabled me to relive my life so far and to experience once more in the depths of my soul the unbelievable miracle that is the story of the Jewish people over the ages. My wife and children and grandchildren have remained my joy and support over the time and effort required to write this book. In fact, I must admit that I wrote with my grandchildren and great-grandchildren in mind, for it is to them and their generation to correctly assess the patterns of Jewish history, avoid previous grievous social and policy errors, and preserve the glory of Torah and Israel.

Berel Wein
Jerusalem
Kislev 5771, December 2010

Chapter One

Does History Really Repeat Itself?

This chapter should properly be entitled "Need History Really Repeat Itself?" Common wisdom asserts that one must learn from history – in other words, the past is a useful and accurate guide to the present and to future events as well. Yet the nature of people and governments is to pretty much ignore this apparently simple wisdom. The same mistakes that were made centuries ago in personal lives and national policies are repeated again in the blissful hope that somehow now these failed policies and wrong behavior will work. Thus the pattern of wrong policy and behavior followed by disaster followed by recovery, and then followed by the cycle of wrong policy and behavior again, disaster, recovery etc., is firmly established in the story of humans and institutions. If insanity is truly defined as following disastrous policies over and over again in the forlorn hope that somehow this time those policies will work out successfully, then we all truly live in an officially insane world. For the nature of all humans, and Jews are no exception, is to consciously repeat past errors of judgment, policy and behavior. I think that is what the rabbis of the Talmud meant when they stated that one does not commit sin unless possessed by a spirit of foolishness and near insanity. The wonderful historian and author Barbara Tuchman wrote a gem of a book called *The March of Folly*. That book, covering millennia of human history, clearly shows the mistakes of national policy that were repeated over and over again throughout the centuries in every climate and clime. Human folly is not restricted by location or creed, nor by time or circumstance.

One need only study the books of the Bible to become aware of this human trait. The Jewish people in biblical times always were backsliding into paganism, divisiveness, and false alliances with neighboring powers. The constant and inexorable disasters that followed were later always followed by periods of repentance and restoration of Jewish values as though the Jewish people had learned its lesson and now would continue forward on its God-given path of holiness and dedication to the Lord and humanity. But a generation or two later, the previous lesson was forgotten or ignored and this cycle of waywardness, foolishness, disaster and revitalization would repeat itself anew. This seemingly insane behavior is not restricted to biblical times or the people of Israel. For a current example, the policies of the Western world toward aggressors, terrorism, anti-Semitism and totalitarianism are starkly reminiscent of those exact same policies that took place in the 1930s in the disastrous lead up to World War II. Then, these policies were called "appeasement," and today they are called "engagement." But a rose by any other name is still a rose, this time a putrid one. And this rose has wilted prematurely many times before in the human story. The pattern of Jewish history therefore reflects this biblical story in all times and localities.

In the world of finance and economics the boom-and-bust cycle is well known and oft repeated. Such cycles have repeated themselves in all centuries of the modern era. Yet every time the bust phase occurs, the experts and we ordinary mortals are shocked, surprised and confused. I remember hearing one of the great financial gurus of the time state in a radio interview when the NASDAQ index reached 5000 that this was its correct valuation. Of course the NASDAQ since has declined by over fifty percent but that financial guru is still giving out sage advice to people who choose to forget or ignore his very mistaken statement a generation earlier. Comrade Stalin and Chairman Mao, Fidel Castro and

Pol Pot no longer exist but the radical Left still idealizes them in spite of the hundreds of millions that they killed in bringing about the "new better world" that somehow never quite arrived. Thus North Korea, Syria, Iran, Venezuela and others still remain the darlings of the Left and are encouraged in their vicious totalitarianism by the forgetful humanists who want to see only good in a world that unfortunately does not conform in reality to their illusions and wishful thinking. Thus the cycle of cruelty, death, failure, rehabilitation and recovery common to all human societies continues unabated.

In the Jewish world the pattern of abandonment of Torah and its observances, followed by assimilation, self-hatred, disasters, and later resurgence of Torah beliefs again can clearly be traced throughout Jewish history. In the later chapters of this book regarding acculturation and assimilation as well as the chapter regarding messianism, these patterns will be traced for the reader in greater detail. Suffice it to say that for now this pattern is omnipresent in the story of the Jewish people. Part of the problem in breaking this vicious cycle is the blind refusal of much of Jewish society, in the entire variety of the spectrum of this society, to even recognize the existence of such a pattern in Jewish life and, therefore, it becomes impossible to learn any of the lessons of the past and not to continue to repeat those errors over and over again. If one does not recognize or remember past recurring problems then there certainly cannot be any current solutions to the difficulties that afflict us. The patterns that exist in Jewish history are evident only to those that wish to examine them objectively. It is not so much a matter of belief and ideology that should govern us as it is a matter of clear thinking and recognizing reality. If such recognition truly takes place then there is excellent hope that history need not ever eternally repeat itself in our society. The Talmud teaches us that the words of the great Hebrew prophets that were written down in scrolls and preserved for us in books were so written and preserved because they have validity in all generations. They point out the major and difficult problems that afflicted Jewish life in the past, recommend solutions to those problems, and warn about repeating those errors in the future. Since the problems are recurrent ones, the words of the prophets should be studied and internalized in every age and situation. History certainly does repeat itself, but it need not do so always. Common sense and a little less insanity can prevent the recurrence of the cycle of continuing disaster and then forced rebirth in Jewish national and personal life.

The departure of much of eastern European Ashkenazic Jewry from Jewish observance and tradition – the creation of the so-called secular Jew – occurred in the nineteenth and early twentieth century in eastern Europe itself. A major factor that propelled this mass desertion from Jewish tradition was the state of Jewish society at that time. Overwhelming poverty, fractured and bitter divisions within the general and in particular the religious Jewish world, the refusal to deal with an increasingly unfair social hierarchy, all reflected in religious Jewish life of that time and place, combined to alienate the younger generations from their heritage and faith. False gods, such as Marxism and secular Zionism, made grandiose promises and ignited inspirational dreams. The Torah leaders of the time, for various reasons of societal circumstance, were unable to match the promises of these false gods. Preaching poverty as a permanent way of life and having a one-size-fits-all, very limited educational system proved to be a very unattractive way of life for millions of Jews. Jews voted with their feet, fleeing that society and way of life and immigrating to new shores which would prove to be more hospitable physically but more dangerous spiritually. They also voted with their intellect, minds and new beliefs. Humanism, socialism, nationalism, militant labor unionism and complete assimilation into the non-Jewish world all proved themselves to be initially more attractive than a faith-based society that was viewed as being desperately poor, to a great extent uneducated and backward, and riven with factionalism. Yet somehow this pattern is being repeated again in sections of the Jewish religious world two centuries later. In over glorifying everything in the past, including unfortunately its errors, mistakes and defeats, we guarantee that the same sad results will inevitably occur once more. Eventually, history is unforgiving and thus repeats itself.

A final word, if I may, regarding history repeating itself. In democratic societies when popular elections take place regularly – people are running for office continually – it is de rigueur for politicians campaigning for office to propose change, hope, and easy solutions to often intractable problems. Almost all of the time this leads to unreasonable expectations, and when elected, almost inevitably to a repetition of past policies and ideas that have failed and thus to a continuation of the cycle and pattern described above. Resurrecting past policies by giving them new names is a well known political habit of governments. Many times leaders convince themselves that they really have new breakthrough solutions to old problems without realizing that they are really reinventing the wheel, and more often than not a broken wheel at that. Very rarely has this type of essentially recycled programming and initiative been successful. Yet the nature of the beast is to continue with this type of process. Thus a realization of the past and a determination not to repeat its follies and errors is a necessary requirement of governmental, social, religious and communal life. The patterns in history do repeat themselves for good or for better. Being aware of them is already a small but essential victory in the campaign for a better society.

Chapter Two

Acculturation and Assimilation

There are definite dangers in being a small people. The Torah promised us at the beginning of our story that we would never be a numerous people – in fact that we would be the smallest of all peoples. One would think that as long as we are in our country and isolated society we are safe from outside influences. However that would not be an accurate assessment of the real world. A small people, a continual minority amongst the many, is always faced with the dangers of outside, dominant cultural influences, physical assimilation and eventual disappearance.

From the first day of our existence as a people we were influenced by the other nations and cultures that existed in that area of the world. Centuries of life and decades of slavery in Egypt left their mark on the Jewish people. Many commentators are of the opinion that the generation of those who left Egypt did not enter the land of Israel because they could not shake off the influence of Egyptian culture and its pagan values in their lives. Throughout the story of the Jews in the desert of Sinai we continually hear the refrain "back to Egypt" sounded whenever problems and difficulties arise. The generation of the desert therefore can be seen as somehow being Egyptians of the Mosaic persuasion. This is in spite of the fact that this generation was known as being a *dor de'a* – a generation of wisdom and holy knowledge, the generation that stood at Sinai and accepted the eternal Torah on behalf of the eternal people. We see in the Torah how the Jews were influenced by the hypocritical blessings of Balaam, how they were seduced by the daughters of Midian, how they reverted to Egyptian paganism at the incident of the Golden Calf, and how they suffered both military victories and defeats at the hands of the Canaanites and Amalek. Thus, from the beginnings of our becoming a people, the Jews were always affected by the processes of acculturation and assimilation. Acculturation was necessary in order to allow Jewish life to exist and even flourish in an exile dominated by non-Jewish inimical powers. Acculturation occurs regarding dress, language, secular studies, systems and methods of education, food, mannerisms and societal mores. Assimilation however reflects a deep desire to be less Jewish and to blend in completely with the surrounding environment and society. It reflects the willingness to give up Jewish particularism in favor of being a part of the general whole. Assimilation doomed and dooms Jews to eventual demographic extinction. And this is a constant pattern in Jewish history – the struggle against assimilation and disappearance while somehow Judaizing and accepting and dealing with acculturation.

Throughout the biblical period as recorded for us in the Tanakh the influence of the pagan neighbors and societies on the Jewish kingdoms of Judah and Israel was profound and continuing. In spite of all of the warnings of the prophets of Israel of the impending disasters that following the value systems and mores of the surrounding pagan societies would bring, the Jews could not break out of this ring of intense acculturation. Even the most righteous kings of Judah were unable to completely stem this tide of pagan culture, practice and values. Marriages of political and diplomatic convenience were consummated between the Jewish royal houses and the royal families of the non-Jewish neighboring empires, all of which led to assimilation and physical and spiritual disaster. Eventually the northern kingdom of Israel – the Ten Tribes – was carried off into a never-ending exile by Assyria, and the southern kingdom of Judah and Jerusalem and its holy Temple were destroyed by the Babylonian empire. Carried off to Babylonian exile, the generation of the time refused to acculturate let alone assimilate. They bit off the tips of their thumbs rather than play the songs of Zion on their harps for the amusement of their Babylonian captors. But soon Jews became more comfortable in their new Babylonian homes and society. Eventually there arose a generation of Babylonian Jews that approached the prophet Ezekiel and told him, in effect, we quit! They stated that the Temple is destroyed, there is no longer a Jewish state in the land of Israel, we are comfortably and apparently permanently settled here in Babylonia, we desire to assimilate completely into the host society, so therefore we state "*kekhol hagoyim beit Yisrael,* The house of Israel is to be exactly alike to all of the other nations of the world." The Lord, however, told the prophet that He would not allow that to happen, and soon thereafter the near annihilation of the Jews in the story of Purim proved His point. In the later chapter in this book on anti-Semitism, the role of anti-Semitism in combating assimilation on one hand, and conversely encouraging it on the other hand will be discussed much more fully. Suffice it here to state that anti-Semitism is always a potent force in the story of both Jewish acculturation and assimilation.

Ezra, Nehemiah, and the Men of the Great Assembly found and build the Second Commonwealth in Jerusalem and restore the Temple. The seventy-year Babylonian exile is at an end. Yet most of the Jews of Babylonia remain in Babylonia. Ezra is able to bring less than fifty thousand returnees to the land of Israel. And as the Talmud records for us, the "better" Jews of clear pedigree and wealth remained in Babylonia. Ezra encounters a Jewish population in the land of Israel that is not Sabbath observant and with a great deal of intermarriage with non-Jewish women in its midst. The Samaritans, a group of questionable Jews converted under duress during a plague of lions running amok in the country, claim to be the real Jews, and that Ezra and his people are interlopers and frauds. Facing this drastic situation of assimilation, Ezra and Nehemiah somehow rectify the situation, the Samaritans are faced down and defeated, the non-Jewish women are sent away, the public observance of Sabbath is restored, new laws and decrees to strengthen religious values and observances are adopted, and a new covenant – *berit amana* – is entered into between God and Israel. However, signs of the acculturation of the Jews that occurred while living in Babylonia and Persia are now evident in Jewish life. The names of the Jewish lunar months are now Babylonian in origin, the ancient semi-holy tongue of Aramaic, spoken in Babylonia, becomes the *lingua franca* for much of Second Commonwealth Jewry living in the land of Israel and many domestic customs of Babylonian and Persian life are present in Jewish life as well. Since there is such a large Jewish population still living in Babylonia and Persia that retains intimate and continuing contact with the Jews in the land of Israel, this type of acculturation was readily understood and accepted. All of this would soon change with the coming of the conquering Greeks to the Middle East in c.325 BCE.

Alexander the Great arrives in the land of Israel. He brings with him not only his armies but Greek culture as well. Eventually his armies leave, riven by internal ambitions and disputes. But the wisdom of Aristotle, the language of Homer, the ideas of Greek politics and nascent democracy, the glorification of the human body, the advanced technology of empire, all remain in the land of Israel. And the acculturation of what is called in the Talmud *ḥokhmat Yavanit* – Greek wisdom and culture and values – begins for the Jewish people.

Whereas the pagan cultures of the Canaanites, the Assyrians, the Egyptians and the Babylonians were not viewed as being particularly glorious in their contributions to the progress of human civilization, Greek culture took a quantum leap above these preceding societies. Greek culture embodied drama, art, sports, philosophy, mathematics, aesthetics, political innovations, poetry and literature. It was blinding in its shining appeal. It was the living incarnation of the beauty of Japheth mentioned in the Torah. As such it proved almost irresistible to many Jews. The dark side of Greek culture, its dependence on slavery, its glorification of homosexuality as the highest form of human love, its paganism and rampant immorality in sexual matters, its pantheon of gods and goddesses each more violent and evil than the other, was somehow ignored by many or fully adopted by others. In any event, these groups of Jews who were simply enamored of Greek culture formed a group called the Hellenists, a group which eventually included almost thirty percent of Jews living in the land of Israel and in Egypt as well. This group eventually assimilated completely into Greek culture and beliefs, many of them becoming pagans, avoiding circumcision or even attempting to reverse it on their bodies, and cooperating with the Syrian Greeks ruling the country in suppressing Judaism and persecuting its rabbinic leaders. After the defeat of the Syrian Greeks by the Hasmoneans in c.160 BCE, the Hellenists waned in numbers and influence and eventually morphed themselves into joining the Sadducees, an anti-rabbinic group that denied the divinity of the Oral Law. Nevertheless, there was continual assimilation into Greek (and later, Roman) society and beliefs amongst a significant minority of Jews within the larger Jewish society living in Second Commonwealth times.

If assimilation was obviously present but somehow mainly contained in these times, acculturation took hold in all areas of Jewish life. Greek language appears throughout the Mishna and later the Talmud as well. Greek names abounded in Jewish society and eventually became accepted as being "Jewish" names. Many of the great rabbis of the Mishna bore pure Greek names. The Bible itself was translated into Greek – the Septuagint, *Targum HaShivim* – and the rabbis ascribed to it a miraculous status. Many halakhic terms and norms are described in the Greek word associated with the subject. The rabbis also used Greek medicine, mathematics, astronomy, agriculture, technology and logic in their studies and Torah commentary. Some of the rabbinical students also engaged in the study of *ḥokhmat Yavanit* – most probably Greek philosophy – but apparently not in combination with their Torah studies. But generally speaking, Greek social behavior, values and practices were shunned and abhorred in traditional Jewish society. The difference between acculturation and assimilation is therefore seen clearly in this Jewish attitude toward Greek culture. The Jews of Second Commonwealth times became acculturated, but the majority of them, fiercely loyal to Torah and tradition, never became assimilated.

In Babylonia at the times of the Talmud and the early Geonim (the rabbinic heads of the Babylonian *yeshivot*) around 200–650 CE, the Jews were fully integrated into Babylonian commercial and social life but were in no way assimilated. In fact it is no exaggeration to state that the Jewish world after the completion of the Talmud continues to this day to live a Talmudic lifestyle. Aramaic, the spoken language of Babylonia at that time, in its various dialects became and remains the language of the study of Talmud till today and is part and parcel of modern-day Hebrew as well. But we are unaware of any real assimilationist tendencies or movements within Babylonian Jewry of that time. In the seventh century, Islam arose and conquered Babylonia as well. Originally, Islam set out to convert all of the Jews to its banner and beliefs by the sword. But when it became apparent that the Jews as a whole would not adopt this new faith of Mohammed, Muslims and Jews reached an accommodation whereby the Jews certainly became acculturated in Muslim society but never assimilated in any significant numbers. For assimilation then meant conversion and even the most acculturated Jews were always loath to consider such a radical departure from the faith of their ancestors and its traditions.

The main acculturation in Jewish life in the Muslim world occurred during the "golden age" of Spanish Jewry from the seventh to the twelfth centuries. Arabic then became the spoken language of Spanish Jews though Hebrew experienced a revival amongst the scholars and poets of the Jewish world of the time. Jews adopted Arab medicine, originally Greek in origin; Arabic poetry and literature, music and melody; Arabic dress; participated in the politics and courts of the rulers of the time and in the armies of the rulers of the country; and were deeply embedded in all areas of Spanish Muslim society. Nevertheless, they did not assimilate, for again, assimilation meant conversion and that was outside the pale of Jewish thought and behavior. The Jews of Spain were much influenced by the advanced Muslim culture of the time. They studied all forms of science and philosophy. The reputation of Jewish doctors having extraordinary healing skills and knowledge of pharmacology and medicinal herbs was a product of Jewish life in Spain. The greatest exemplar of the Jewish Torah scholar, philosopher, medical healer and leader of Spanish Jewry is naturally Rabbi Moshe ben Maimon (Rambam, Maimonides). However it is with him that the Spanish "golden age" certainly ends. In 1150 the fanatical Almohad believers in Islam conquered much of Spain and many Jews were forcibly converted, many others brutally executed and still others exiled. In the next century the Christian Reconquest of Spain began and the last three hundred years of Spanish Jewry were years of decline and repression. Even under Christian rule, with the success of the Reconquest, and with its accompanying unrelenting efforts to force the Jews to convert, Jewish philosophers and doctors flourished. Rabbi Moshe ben Naḥman (Ramban, Nahmanides), Don Isaac Abrabanel and Rabbi Yosef Albo are only three of the many examples of the process of acculturation that continued in Jewish society even in Christian Spain and even in the times of the murderous, Church-inspired and enforced Inquisition. But this process of acculturation in Jewish life now met determined foes within Jewish society itself.

The central point person in this conflict was the Rambam, Rabbi Moshe ben Maimon, himself. His work of philosophy, *Moreh Nevukhim* (*The Guide for the Perplexed*), and his philosophical chapters in his grand masterpiece of halakha, *Mishneh Torah,* raised a storm of protest among certain sections of Provencal and Spanish Jewry. This dispute flared for half a century and eventually resulted in the burnings of these works by the Church at the instigation of Jewish zealots and hotheads. Even though the dispute died down, the approach to acculturation hardened significantly. After the exile of the Jews from Spain many rabbinic leaders, both Sephardic and Ashkenazic, attributed this disaster to the willingness of Spanish Jewry over the centuries to acculturate itself within the general Spanish society. However, the truth be said, acculturation occurred in Ashkenazic society as well. It is certainly true that the Ashkenazic world also absorbed acculturation although in a much more limited fashion than its Sephardic brethren. Rashi (Rabbi Shlomo Yitzḥaki, eleventh-century France), in his commentaries to Torah and Talmud, uses French words liberally. Jews were very active in the commerce of the time especially in the fields of banking and money lending and exchanging, wine producing, and all types of crafts and trades. However, since the non-Jewish society in France and Germany was basically ignorant, illiterate and light-years behind the culture of the Muslims of the time, this was reflected in Ashkenazic Jewish society as well with almost no interest in poetry (except for liturgy and lamentations), medicine, the arts or science. Mathematics and astronomy were known to Ashkenazic Jews but basically from Talmudic and traditional sources exclusively. Thus, acculturation was severely limited, while assimilation as such was unknown short of actual forced conversion to Christianity. In general, it may be said that Ashkenazic Jewry in the Middle Ages was much less influenced by the surrounding society and therefore not as open to acculturation as were the Sephardic Jews of the time. Of course a great deal of this is due not only to Jewish attitudes, but to the overwhelmingly hostile environment toward Jews that medieval European Christian society fostered. When the non-Jewish world attempts to completely shut out the Jews from their society and lives, there is little room for assimilation or even much acculturation to take place. The open hostility of the Christian European society to Jews and Judaism forcibly insulated much of medieval Jewish society from any form of acculturation. Only when the outside society becomes more tolerant and accepting of a Jewish presence in its midst does the pattern of Jewish acculturation and the danger of assimilation resume.

In the sixteenth century, a sizable number of Spanish Jews settled in the Netherlands and helped create the thriving metropolis of Amsterdam. A large number of Sephardic Jews immigrated to Turkey. There they used and developed a previously known distinctive language – Ladino – which was a combination of Spanish, Arabic and Hebrew. The Jews of Turkey created a strong community and, though much acculturation took place, were loyal and traditional Jews. Holland was more liberal toward its Jews than Turkey though discrimination and bigotry against them certainly existed there. From famous works of art of the Dutch painters of the time it is apparent that Jews became acculturated early and easily in that environment. They spoke Dutch, dressed (including the rabbis) like the non-Jewish nobles and burghers of the time, and were very active in commerce, thereby helping Holland to become a world colonial empire. Jews were also patrons of the arts and supported many of the great Dutch masters including Rembrandt. The number of Jewish scenes painted by him testifies to the Jewish presence and influence in the Amsterdam of his day. Holland was overwhelmingly Protestant and therefore the horrors of the Inquisition disappeared. Jews traveled and settled in the newly established colonies of the Dutch West Indies and the Jewish presence in Curacao and other West Indian islands was strong and influential. In fact, it was from these islands that the first Jews, all Sephardic in origin and practice, arrived on the shores of North America. Eventually some of these Jews assimilated as well, intermarrying and losing their Jewish identity. However, the vast majority of Dutch Jewry, though certainly acculturated, remained loyal and observant Jews. They were the Jews who began to return to England in the late seventeenth and eighteenth centuries, becoming acculturated there but still retaining their Jewish identity and practices. They faced great discrimination but not outright persecution there. In colonial times in America there were relatively few Jews in the country. The range of discrimination against them depended upon which of the colonies they settled in, but essentially they enjoyed relative freedom and even acceptance in the new world that was being created there on the basis of equality for all, and freedom of and from religion.

In Renaissance Italy, Jews were deeply acculturated and adopted the dress and manners of the general population. From rabbinic responsa of the time we can easily see that the social mores and practices were adopted generally by Italian Jewry, often to the disapproval and consternation of their rabbinic leaders. Since many of these rabbis were eastern European Jews in origin and outlook, their reaction against the extreme acculturation of Italian Jewry is understandable though they were apparently futile in strongly influencing their congregants in these matters. Italian Jewry remained fiercely loyal to Judaism though they were completely acculturated into Italian society. This was in spite of the creation of the ghetto in Venice in the sixteenth century to separate Jews from the general society. In fact the creation of the ghetto itself testifies to the fact that the Jews were so integrated in Venetian and Italian life that the Church and the local governments felt threatened by their presence and influence. The ghetto helped remind the Jews that their presence and status in Italy was fragile. But nevertheless, Italian Jewry continued to function, completely acculturated but not assimilated. Italian Jewry had its own form of liturgy and customs and was fiercely loyal to them. As mentioned above, many of its rabbinic leaders came from Poland and Central Europe (such as Rabbi Yehuda Mintz [the Mahari Mintz of Padua], and Rabbi Me'ir Katzenellenbogen [the Maharam of Padua] and others) and they also underwent the process of acculturation, though they strongly warned of the dangers of assimilation that they felt lurked below the surface of Italian Jewish life. Another anomaly of Italian Jewish life was the institution of the "Pope's Jews." This group of Jews lived in Rome under the express protection of the Pope and the

Church. These Jews were meant to be preserved as witnesses to the perfidy of the Jews in not recognizing the Christian savior and to witness his second coming. The Church strongly protested to the Germans the deportation of these Jews to Auschwitz in World War II while having been silent on the killing of millions of other Jews by the very same Germans. There always seemed to be a difference in non-Jewish eyes throughout Jewish history between Jews generally and "my good Jews who are not like the others."

Eastern European Jewry also became acculturated. Its spoken language was Yiddish, a corrupted form of German interspersed with Polish, Hebrew, and Slavic words. The Jews did not speak the language of the countries in which they lived in eastern Europe amongst themselves; Yiddish was the permanent lingua franca of the people. Yet in dress, mannerisms, food, music and commerce, Jews became acculturated in Lithuania, Poland, Ukraine and later Russia. Ashkenazic Jewry of eastern Europe developed its own liturgy and customs, which differed materially from those of western Europe, Germany and certainly the Sephardim. Jews enjoyed a certain amount of internal autonomy for a number of centuries (late fifteenth till early eighteenth century) in eastern Europe establishing its own governing body known as the Council of the Four Lands (Congress Poland, Galicia, Ukraine, Volhynia, and later Lithuania). This enabled the Jewish community to live in a sort of splendid isolation at least regarding all internal matters of its life and society. Thus even though acculturation existed and pervaded many aspects of Jewish life, it was perhaps mostly unnoticed by the Jews themselves. Jews then lived mainly in small villages – the *shtetl* – and thus there was no strong desire among eastern European Jews to resemble or copy the life style of their illiterate, violent, alcoholic non-Jewish neighbors. Assimilation was therefore not a great threat to these communities, though there were always some defections from traditional Jewish life in all ages and in all places. For a number of centuries, eastern European Jewry was able to wrap itself in a protective cocoon that allowed for acculturation but admitted little threat of assimilation. From the eighteenth century onwards until its destruction in World War II, all of this would change as the pattern of history again rose to change the present and the future.

The ideas of the Enlightenment, the rise of Protestantism in

Europe and the discoveries of new continents and resultant colonialism, all combined to bring about a change in the status of Jews in Europe, especially in western Europe. The successes of the American and French revolutions, the spread of the ideas of Western liberalism through Napoleon's armies and the gradual victory of Parliament over the King in England, collectively helped to free Jews from the prison of ghetto walls and to allow them at least limited entry into general society. Ironically, the country that allowed Jews to proceed most rapidly toward equal participation in society in the eighteenth and nineteenth centuries was Germany, under the leadership of Prussia and its emperors. Thus, the Jews living there, who always were somewhat acculturated, became even more so, giving up Yiddish to speak pure German and attending German schools. Moses Mendelssohn was the champion of this wave of strong push for maximum German acculturation. However, this type of acculturation almost immediately led to assimilation and conversion to Christianity. Most of Mendelssohn's own children converted, and his descendants in the next generation were almost uniformly all Christian. The Reform movement then arose in Germany, partially to stem the tide of conversions. It radically changed Judaism to fit then current German mores. Saturday became Sunday, most of the observances of Judaism were done away with, an organ was installed in their temples, Hebrew was eliminated in favor of German in the prayer services, Zion and Jerusalem were eliminated from the aspirations and goals of the Jewish people and it espoused the idea of Jews no longer identifying themselves as Jews but rather as "Germans of the Mosaic persuasion." All of this did not arrest complete assimilation and conversions but instead encouraged them. Heinrich Heine, one of the noted Jewish apostates of the nineteenth century whose self-hatred of himself often translated into overt anti-Semitism, famously stated: "Christianity is the ticket for admittance into European society." Tens of thousands of Jews were willing to purchase that ticket. Thus a wave of assimilation and conversions swept the western and central European Jewish world in the nineteenth century. The biblical pattern of rising (and later waning) assimilation stretching through all of the previous generations of Jewish history was thus now repeated in a more modern, nineteenth-century form.

Traditional Jewry in Germany fought back against this wave of assimilation and resultant conversions by adopting almost complete acculturation, but Judaizing it. Rabbis Yaakov Etlinger (author of the great Talmudic commentary *Arukh LaNer*), Ḥakham Isaac Bernays, Samson Raphael Hirsch, Seligman Baer Bamberger (author of *Yad HaLevi*), Azriel Hildesheimer, David Tzvi Hoffman and others, led this nineteenth-century, German-Jewish movement in differing degrees and localities but with a general common strategy of allowing Jews to be full participants in German society without having to compromise their sacred beliefs and Torah observances. Hirsch translated the Torah into impeccable German and supplied a brilliant commentary to it, also in German. He built a model community in Frankfurt am Main of Jews engaged fully in German financial, professional and academic life who were nevertheless meticulously observant of Jewish law and ritual. So to speak, he beat the Reform movement at its own game, disproving the idea that assimilation was the only way to enter and prosper in nineteenth-century German society. Hildesheimer established a rabbinic seminary in Berlin that combined intensive Talmudic and rabbinic studies with broad secular knowledge and public skills. Hoffman authored a great work of rabbinic and halakhic responsa – *Melamed LeHo'il* – while authoring at the same time a commentary to Torah that demolished the specious theories of biblical criticism that had gained fashion (and unfortunately still exist today – ironically, mainly in Jewish academic circles) at that time. Orthodoxy in Germany, especially in the smaller communities, recovered strongly from the onslaught of Reform. It was an outstanding example of the triumph of the process of allowing acculturation in a traditional form to take hold in the Jewish society thus triumphing over outright assimilation and the abandonment of all traditional Torah norms.

In eighteenth- and nineteenth-century eastern Europe new movements arose to change the traditional rhythms of Jewish life that had existed there for centuries. The Hasidic movement, in all its various branches and ideologies, gained great popular support. In so doing, it undermined the traditional authority and role of the rabbis and scholars and substituted for it the authority of the rebbe – the righteous and holy leader of a particular Hasidic sect. Hasidism created its own acculturation with its different nuances of dress, prayer ritual, customs, song and melody. It took the garb of seventeenth-century Russian and Polish nobility and made it Jewish garb. This is especially true regarding the *shtreimel* – a fur-trimmed hat. A variation of this type of hat – a *spodek*, a taller, straighter, all-fur hat – became the dress of certain groups of Hasidim. Lithuanian rabbis also wore these types of fur hats, but in the nineteenth century they mainly wore the frocks and top hats of Western nobility. In England, Germany and France, rabbis wore robes that resembled those of Christian clergymen of the time. However, in eastern Europe, the rabbis refused to apply the acculturation of German Orthodoxy to their congregations. The spoken language remained Yiddish, in the main secular studies were unknown in their educational system, and the Orthodox Jew found almost no entry into the general non-Jewish society, except for the traditional fields of Jewish commerce: the liquor trade, the rent broker between landowners and the serfs and tenant farmers, and money lending. Jews were also commonly porters, water carriers, peddlers, teamsters, and wagon drivers and, toward the end of the century, tailors, shoemakers, and factory workers in the textile trade. Jewish poverty was rampant in eastern Europe as was a high rate of infant and child mortality. Living conditions were miserable. Assimilation meant conversion, something which Jews in eastern Europe, unlike their German and Austrian brethren, refused to countenance in any substantial numbers. The ideas of Western Enlightenment found expression in the movement of *Haskala*, which promised to alleviate Jewish suffering and soften governmental anti-Semitism. *Haskala* failed to accomplish either of these two goals and gradually led to a disregard for Torah observances and Jewish tradition amongst its adherents. Hasidism vehemently opposed all ideas of *Haskala* and was in turn opposed and vilified by the adherents of *Haskala*. *Haskala* was an attempt to create a new kind of acculturation – a Jewish acculturation through the creation of a Jewish culture to substitute for Torah and religious observance. This type of acculturation in many instances led to complete assimilation and the defection of its adherents from Jewish life completely over the space of a few generations.

In one of the great ironies of Jewish history, the assimilation of German Jewry in the nineteenth and twentieth centuries only exacerbated the barely latent anti-Semitism of that society. Amos Elon's book,

The Pity of It All, doggedly traces this tragic descent to the Holocaust. In eastern Europe the attempts of *Haskala* to neutralize the anti-Semitism of the Czar and his court also met with dismal failure. The modern, sophisticated well-read Jew of the nineteenth century was in many ways despised more by Russian society than was his *shtetl*-bred, caftan-clad brother. In the face of this, many conversions took place amongst this "elite" group of Jews, an act of personal desperation at their failure to otherwise ingratiate themselves with the non-Jewish society. Movements of acculturation arose in eastern European society in an attempt to stabilize and improve Jewish life. In the religious world, the *Musar* movement, founded by Rabbi Yisrael Lipkin of Salant, incorporated within it Western-style dress, punctiliousness of time and appearance, ethical behavior between people and a sense of tolerance for others, introspection and psychological insight, a demand for greater personal spirituality, and a penetrating analysis of classical Jewish texts. This movement took hold mainly in the Lithuanian yeshivot of the time but sadly is of little influence today in the twenty-first century. This type of acculturation as exemplified by the *Musar* movement is, in reality, an attempt to return to Jewish basics and to shed some of the layers of the non-Jewish acculturation assembled in our long exile and dispersion among the nations and cultures of the world. It is an attempt to "return our crown to its ancient luster." Thus, many times it is possible paradoxically to return to our original selves by the process of positive acculturation of Jewish values that were somehow preserved in the non-Jewish world around us.

In the nineteenth and twentieth centuries, acculturation and assimilation came about through ideals and ideas that gained popularity and policy in the non-Jewish world. Enlightenment, Marxism in all of its virulent forms, nationalism, imperialism, colonialism, theories about social evolution and master races, all gained wide currency in the Europe of their day and all of them penetrated the Jewish world as well. The Bund (the large and powerful anti-religious labor union), secular and labor Zionism, *Haskala,* anarchism and impractical resettlement plans to solve the "Jewish problem" all ravaged the Jewish society of the time. Most of them led to complete assimilation of millions of Jews within two generations, though the success of Zionism in establishing a Jewish state in the land of Israel proved to be a strong brake against assimilation though certainly not to acculturation. By the early twenty-first century, all of these ideologies mentioned above largely disappeared from Jewish society but very few new ideals arose to fill the void. Acculturation now took place through the pursuit of wealth, entertainment and professional sports. All sectors of Jewry were thus acculturated, especially the large Jewish community living in the United States. The acceptance of Jews into American society in the latter half of the twentieth century created a situation that Jews in America no longer felt themselves to be a minority but rather as full Americans, members of the majority American population. This in spite of the fact that numerically, Jews are a very small percentage of the American population, much smaller in number than those groupings that still consider themselves legally and socially to be minorities. This Jewish mindset of full acceptance in American society, echoed by a great many non-Jewish Americans as well, has led to drastic assimilation and intermarriage within Jewish society. The bitter rule of history seems to be that when non-Jews are willing to marry Jews in the absence of any social stigma in so doing, there will also be Jews who are willing to intermarry. This is especially true for Jews who have little Jewish education, are non-observant and do not have connections to Jewish family traditions. The American Jewish community is thus clearly acculturated in all of its sections, but half of it is assimilated while the other half is becoming more and more committed to Jewish tradition, observances and education. The fact that at many American professional sports stadiums and arenas there are public announcements that *Minḥa* (afternoon) or *Ma'ariv* (evening) prayer services will take place at a certain section of the stadium or arena, or that strictly kosher foods are available for purchase, only shows the depth of acculturation in American Jewry. The great accomplishment of American Jewish life – exemplified for instance by Senator Joseph Lieberman's (an Orthodox, observant Jew) near successful run for Vice-President of the United States – is the ability to become completely acculturated without becoming assimilated. Perhaps in no other time and place in the story of the Jewish exile (except maybe Spain's "golden age") has this achievement been realized. The Jewish community in America is still relatively new in the country, historically speaking, so that no permanent conclusions regarding its ultimate fate are now in order. Yet, I think that it should be obvious to all that until now, the American Jewish experience has been unique in the annals of the Jewish Diaspora and exile.

In the modern-day State of Israel, the acculturation to a combination of a traditional yet apparently secular society that is composed partly of socialistic, bureaucratic, Western-values oriented, capitalistic, hedonistic, deeply and rigorously observant, and technologically advanced ideals, has been difficult. However, that this acculturation has occurred is evident in the Israeli personality common to all sectors of the populace, for good or better, and in the modern spoken and written Hebrew language which is pervasive across its polyglot population. Israel is heavily influenced by Western, especially American, cultural norms and ideas. The culture of the Middle East itself and its Arab population has not made as lasting a dent in the Israeli psyche or way of life. Even the midday nap and store closing that was part of Israeli culture a few decades ago has given way to all-day store openings and afternoon naps restricted mainly to Shabbat. Classic assimilation in Israel is almost unknown even though there are many vociferous anti-religious organizations, politicians and individuals in the country. Nevertheless, most of the country eats kosher food and marries halakhically, the cycle of the Jewish calendar and its holidays is fully observed, and Jewish customs, speech and mannerisms permeate everyday life. In the United States for instance, the holiday of Shavuot is almost non-existent except in observant society. Not so in Israel where the dairy companies sell thirty-five percent of their annual cheese and other dairy-products output for Shavuot and constantly advertise the advent of this holiday for weeks before its arrival. Acculturated as it may be, life in Israel is a Jewish life in all facets of existence. Even if many Jews in Israel are not observant, basically the vast majority of Jews living in Israel are religious. They believe in the existence and benevolence of the God of Israel. And that is probably the greatest barrier to assimilation that exists.

The pattern of acculturation and assimilation is clear in the Jewish story. Acculturation is apparently unavoidable since Jews are so small in number compared to the rest of the world's population. But acculturation need not necessarily lead to assimilation. However, not recognizing that acculturation always occurs and pretending that nothing has changed in Jewish life and society for the past thousands of years leaves us vulnerable to an acculturation that will lead to assimilation. The inability to deal with and recognize the distinctive nature of American life and society led to the creation of different schisms and groupings within the Jewish American society, and these in turn have led down the slippery slope of assimilation and intermarriage. History's patterns constantly reappear before us. Dealing with them successfully, honestly and realistically is the key to Jewish survival and healthy continuity.

Chapter Three

Torah Study

The study of Torah has been the mainstay, not only of Jewish scholarship over the ages, but of Jewish life and society as well. The Talmud ranks Torah study as being the equal of all other Torah commandments and values. The Jewish attitude was that study for study's sake alone was of great value in itself, especially since the Talmud also taught us that study inevitably influences behavior and performance of positive actions. However, Torah study, like the subject itself, has an infinite quality to it. There is basic Torah study for all Jews and there is Torah study for the elite scholars. There are those whose sole occupation in life is studying, teaching and writing about Torah subjects. There are the others, the vast majority of the Jewish people, who engage in work and professions and nonetheless find some time for daily Torah study. Judaism was always a religion that demanded literacy from its adherents and therefore Torah education remained a requirement of Jewish life from one's earliest age to the end of one's life and was the accepted norm of all Jewish societies and ages. However, the graph of Torah study in Jewish history is not one consistent line on the grid. Also, the methodology and organization of Torah study differed in varying communities and eras. Though the subject matter of the Torah remained the constant, the other variables of schools, teachings, methods, language and analysis were subject to change and great variations. Therefore, different patterns regarding the mechanisms of Torah study itself are easily discerned in the long story of the Jewish people.

The generation of Moses, the generation that actually accepted the Torah and its challenges and responsibilities was called in Jewish tradition the *dor de'a* – the generation of intellect and knowledge. This generation, living for decades in a miraculous Godly cocoon, protected from the elements, sustained by manna from heaven and the well of Miriam, was able to devote itself to the study of Torah on a full-time basis. From the Torah itself we see that Moses taught Torah – the principles and explanations of the Oral Law as well as the Written Law as it unfolded – to the priests, the Levites, the Sanhedrin court and through them to all of the masses of Israel. The Torah also emphasizes that the preferable method of Jewish education was what today is called home schooling. Mothers and fathers teaching their children, grandparents teaching grandchildren – that seems to be the literal understanding of the Torah's commandment regarding Jewish education. We have no record as to what sort of formal educational system if any existed during the period of Joshua and the Judges of Israel. The Talmud pointed out that Joshua himself was subject to angelic criticism because of the neglect of his own personal study of Torah during the battles for Jericho and Ai. In fact we have little knowledge of the system of education in First Temple times generally. The people were taught by the prophets, who were the ultimate transmitters of the Oral Law and of the Torah knowledge and values of Sinai. There were very many prophets during the time of the First Temple, far more than the number whose words are actually transcribed for us in the canon of the Bible itself. The Talmud tells us that during the reign of the holy King Hezekiah of Judah, Jewish Torah knowledge was universal amongst all of the younger children of Israel from "Dan to Beersheba." But how this system of mass, intensive, universal Torah education was achieved and what its formal methodologies were is still unknown to us. The constant swing from observance to the backsliding of paganism that occurred during First Temple times must have had a negative influence on Jewish education generally during those volatile times. Rabbi Reuvein Margolies, in a very novel idea that is characteristic of his great Torah scholarship, theorizes that Torah education, practice and knowledge was very widespread in First Temple times but that the masses somehow reconciled it to the practices of paganism as well!* How that was possible is puzzling to me but it seems there is no limit to Jewish ingenuity and incongruous behavior.

After the demise and disappearance of prophecy, the study of the Oral Law and its scholars came to be the main teachings of Torah study. The development of the Mishna spanned a period of five centuries from the time of the great Ezra till the generation of the holy Rabbi Yehuda HaNasi. This development involved a nationwide creation of schools under the supervision and encouragement of the great men of the Mishna. This guaranteed a basic Jewish education and literacy to all. However, there were different approaches to higher Jewish education during this period. Rabban Gamliel II posted guards at the door of the yeshiva of the Sanhedrin that he headed to prevent students deemed insincere from entering. When Rabban Gamliel II was temporarily deposed by his colleagues from the leadership of the Sanhedrin and its yeshiva, he was replaced by Rabbi Elazar ben Azaria, who removed the guards at the entrance and allowed all who wished to enter to do so. On that day the Talmud tells us that "many benches were added in the study hall." In reality these two conflicting attitudes existed within the scholars of the Mishna almost from the beginning of the era. In the book of *Avot* (Ethics of the Fathers) we read that Yose ben Yoezer said that one's home and place of study should be open to "scholars and the wise." However, his colleague Yose ben Yoḥanan stated that one's house and place of study should be open wide for everyone. Shammai and the school that he founded were rigorous and demanding in admitting students to his study hall. Hillel had a much more lenient attitude and therefore his school was almost always in the majority in deciding halakhic issues. Thus whether higher Torah study was meant for the masses of Israel or only for the elite remains a question in Jewish life throughout the ages, and shifting patterns regarding this important policy-attitude continue in almost every era of Jewish history.

There is a general disdain expressed by the Talmud for those who

* Reuvein Margolies, *HaMikra VeHaMesora* (Jerusalem: Mosad HaRav Kook, 1964).

are deemed ignorant of Jewish law and lore. However, from the anecdotes of the Talmud it seems that most of the Jews were far from scholarly, both in the land of Israel and in Babylonia. The great yeshiva of Sura in Babylonia at the time of Rav (c.230 CE) numbered twelve hundred students and it was the largest school of its type existent then. There was, however, a period of two months a year (Adar and Elul) devoted to mass study – the *yarkhei kalla*. During these months, thousands of Jews attended the yeshivot of Babylonia to hear the Torah lectures of the scholars of the time. The Talmud states that when this immense crowd arose from hearing the lecture the dust of their feet created a cloud that could be seen from a great distance away. The Talmud was a product of almost four centuries of scholarship and many hundreds of contributors and scholars, but from the Talmud itself it seems that the masses did not really appreciate or participate in the creation of this great book. Rava (c.320 CE) complained that in his home town the people showed insufficient respect to the Torah scholars and scholarship. It seems that the masses of Israel at that time were mainly observant but hardly scholarly, while at the top of the society there existed a thin layer of highly intelligent and creative Torah scholars whose lives and achievements are outlined for us in the Talmud. With the destruction of the Jewish communities in the land of Israel in the fourth and fifth centuries, Jewish life in Babylonia became the primary paradigm for all Jewish life throughout the Mediterranean basin. Thus, for the next few centuries, a rather uneducated though observant and Jewishly loyal laity, and a rarefied yet supremely intellectually gifted and scholarly upper strata of Jewish society became the norm in Jewish life.

This was especially true regarding Sephardic Jewry centered in Spain, North Africa and Portugal, and to some extent, Provencal Jewry as well. The Jewish communities in Provence were very small – Lunel, the largest Jewish community in Provence only had three hundred Jews residing there according to the twelfth-century traveler Benjamin of Tudela – and where there was a small Jewish population, the scholars and rabbis were naturally a disproportionately large percentage of the population. Spain and Portugal had large Jewish populations and there the masses were not great Torah scholars while the rabbis were. The Spanish scholars had a bent for poetry and introduced many songs and poems into the prayer liturgy. They were also great Hebrew grammarians and they concentrated on this aspect as part of their Torah study curriculum in their commentaries to the Torah. As to their study of the Talmud, at least until the thirteenth century, they were more interested in the forest – the overall practical application of the halakha as determined by the Talmud – than they were in the trees – the back-and-forth, question-and-answer discussion in the Talmud as to how it arrived at certain halakhic conclusions. Thus the greatest works of the Sephardic world of the early Middle Ages were the commentary of Rabbi Yitzḥak Alfasi (Rif) to the Talmud, which was basically an abridgement of the Talmud reflecting only the halakhic conclusions derived from there, and the *Mishneh Torah* of Maimonides that codified all of Jewish and Talmudic law and attempted to supersede the necessity for studying the Talmud itself. The commentary of Rabbi Menaḥem HaMe'iri to the Talmud reflects the approach of the Provencal scholars in dealing with the subjects of the Talmud on a general and overall basis rather than concentrating on the particular details and meanings of the Talmudic words and phrases themselves. Great halakhic works were written in or translated to Arabic to allow for Torah study by the masses, whose knowledge of Hebrew or Aramaic was limited to prayer. The Sephardic font of writing also became very popular and, in later generations, the printers adopted it for use in the works of Rashi (therefore known until today as Rashi script) and other commentaries to Torah and Talmud.

The foundations for Ashkenazic Jewry were laid in the tenth century in the Rhineland and north-central France. Rabbeinu Gershom, the "Light of the Exile," established a yeshiva in Mainz and the Jewish tri-community of Speyer, Worms and Mainz (acronymed: *Shum*) was the center of Jewish scholarship for a century until its destruction in the First Crusade. The Ashkenazic community was very small, probably no more than five thousand souls, but even its masses were highly educated in Torah studies. The yeshiva in Mainz had a few hundred students, perhaps seven percent of the entire Ashkenazic population of the time. The yeshiva produced the monumental and most beloved scholar Rabbi Solomon Yitzḥaki (Rashi). Rashi's commentary to Torah has remained the classic standby in all Jewish Torah curriculums till our day. But perhaps even more importantly, Rashi's commentary to the Talmud opened up a book that would have remained sealed to the masses of Israel. Because of Rashi's commentary the study of Talmud was widespread in the Ashkenazic world of his day. And his disciples and family continued Rashi's work with the development of the Tosafot that delved into minute detail and analysis on every word, phrase, question, answer and conclusion that appeared on the pages of the Talmud. The Ashkenazic world was far more interested in exploring the trees before moving on to glimpse the forest. Intensive, deeply analytical and creative study of the Talmud became the hallmark of Ashkenazic scholarship and because of its small population base, this type of study and love for it struck deep roots in all later generations of Ashkenazim as well.

The Ashkenazic method of Talmud study soon influenced the Sephardic world. Beginning in the thirteenth century and continuing for the next three centuries, the great Sephardic scholars adopted the methods and analysis of Rashi and Tosafot in their works. The commentaries of Rabbi Moshe ben Naḥman (Ramban), Rabbi Shlomo ben Aderet (Rashba), Rabbi Yonah ibn Gerundi, Rabbi Yom Tov ibn Ashvili (Ritva) Rabbi Nosson ben Reuven (Ran) and other great Sephardic scholars of that era are all written in the style and analytic approach of Tosafot. Though the *Mishneh Torah* of Maimonides remains the pillar of halakhic discourse until our day, his system and organization of Torah study did not take hold in the accepted study of Talmud over the centuries. Rather it was the methodology of Tosafot that became the norm for the study of Talmud, until today when it is now characterized in the yeshivot of our times as being *limud be'iyun* – intensive, analytic study. The more general study of Talmud as characterized in our time by the study of *daf yomi* (a daily page of Talmud) or *bekiut* – a faster, more cursory approach to Talmud study by gaining knowledge of a certain subject matter and avoiding intensive, in-depth analysis – is a departure from the system of Tosafot and resembles, though certainly not exactly, early Sephardic methodology of the study of Talmud. Nevertheless, another offshoot of the organization of Maimonides in the *Mishneh Torah* was the method of Talmudic study pursued in central Europe in the eighteenth and nineteenth centuries called the study of *sugyot* – specific subject matter gathered from many different volumes and places in the Talmud – rather than studying one volume page-by-page in order. So even though the methodology and organization of Tosafot is certainly dominant in the study of Talmud today, it is not monolithic. There are always different patterns that continually reemerge in Torah study and its methodology.

The development of halakha was always through rabbinic responsa. However, beginning with the work of Maimonides in the *Mishneh Torah,* followed by the work of Rabbi Yaakov ben Asher (*Ba'al HaTurim*) in *Arba'a Turim,* and culminating in the works of Rabbi Yosef Caro (*Meḥaber*) in the *Shulḥan Arukh* and Rabbi Moshe Isserles (Rama) in his *Mapa,* organized, systematic, written codes of Jewish law became the basis for halakhic decision. Originally this was contested by many great scholars of the sixteenth century such as Rabbi Shlomo Luria (Maharshal) who felt that these types of written, organized codes of law would stifle Talmudic study and creativity, and limit individual rabbinic decision making as well as undermining the authority of the local rabbi of the community. However, all of these codes of law gained immediate and wide popularity, became the bases of almost all halakhic decision and spawned many other such codes in all of the later centuries of Jewish life. Together with these codes of law, which were given over to intensive study and analysis, rabbinic responsa of individual rabbis on problems and issues of the time continued to flourish. The question then arose as to which – the code of law or the rabbinic responsa – had precedence one over the other when they apparently conflicted in their halakhic decisions. This was especially poignant and personal when the author of the code of law and the author of the rabbinic responsa was one and the same person! The tendency in the rabbinic world always was to rely more on the responsa than on the written code. The written code was, so to speak, theoretical, ivory-tower oriented, detached from real-life experience, while the responsa was personal, real and concerned with actual human beings and therefore worthy of heavenly aid in arriving at halakhic conclusions. The patterns in Jewish history regarding this are evident and changing. We are currently in a pattern of tens and tens of new books of codes of law on all minutiae of Jewish law that are published annually. Great works of rabbinic responsa have not been produced over the past few decades. This situation has helped to account for the rightward turn in many sections of Orthodox Jewish life in the early twenty-first century. In a seminal article published in the

1980s in the journal *Tradition*, Professor Ḥayyim Soloveitchik outlined this shifting pattern from Jewish life being a traditional societal faith to now becoming a book-based religion. All patterns in Jewish history eventually undergo change, so it would be risky to predict whether this emphasis on commentaries to commentaries on Jewish books of code law will continue to dominate Jewish study in the future as well. Suffice it to say that this is a serious issue in terms of Jewish scholarship in all areas of practical Jewish life and society.

The system of Jewish education followed in eastern Europe, and in most of the Sephardic world as well, was that boys entered studies in school, *ḥeder*, or with a private teacher at approximately three years of age. This type of education ended when the child reached the age of ten. The child studied Torah, prophets, Mishna and some elementary Talmud. He also was trained in prayer and in the laws of Shabbat and the Holidays and other practical matters of Jewish law. However, for almost all Jews this was the end of their formal education. Those children (and also those of rabbis, scholars and the wealthier class) that showed special talent and promise, were then allowed to continue their education, especially their Talmudic studies, with the rabbi of the community. Those who continued to show promise in their studies usually then traveled on to a bigger community and studied there with their peers under the direction of famed rabbis and scholars. Because of this winnowing process of education, the dictum of the Talmud that "a thousand enter the study hall but only one emerges to teach and lead" was pretty much the norm in Jewish society. Since there was no alternate system of education available to Jewish children and the Jews lived amidst a basically illiterate non-Jewish society even in the nineteenth century, this type of education was not only accepted but even championed in the Jewish society of the time. All of this was about to change in nineteenth-century life.

As the winds of Emancipation and Enlightenment swept over German and Western Jewry and Reform gained a strong foothold in Jewish society of that time and place, the Jews flocked to obtain a general education, mostly at the expense of the traditional Jewish studies program. As Jews were now allowed to attend universities, the entire thrust of education in these modern societies was on excellence in secular studies. This emphasis would find echoes in the twentieth and twenty-first centuries even in Orthodox circles in England and America when the drive to achieve admittance to Oxford or Harvard would outweigh the need for a more intensive pursuit of traditional Torah studies. Patterns repeat themselves though certainly not always exactly. In Orthodox circles in Germany and England, Jewish studies were now combined with secular studies, whether within the Jewish school or by attendance in non-Jewish schools as well, even to the highest levels of rabbinic seminaries and yeshivot. Rabbi Azriel Hildesheimer's famous Berlin Rabbinical Seminary, founded in the latter half of the nineteenth century, is a prime example of this. The educational system now known to us, of kindergarten to elementary school and then to high school and from there to university, became firmly entrenched in western European Orthodox society. Rabbi Samson Raphael Hirsch's *Realschule* in Frankfurt am Main became the paradigm of Jewish traditional education in western Europe in the nineteenth and twentieth centuries. In fact a higher Torah-study-only yeshiva was not established in Frankfurt until the time of Hirsch's successor and son-in-law Rabbi Solomon Breuer (who was not German but Hungarian by birth.)

In eastern Europe, the heartland of Ashkenazic Jewry, change also occurred. The *Haskala*/Enlightenment challenged the old order of things. In the nineteenth century many *Haskala*-type schools existed in Poland, Lithuania, Ukraine, Hungary, Bohemia and Slovakia. These schools concentrated mainly on teaching Hebrew language, Bible in non-traditional forms, secular studies and, in many instances, Russian or German language and general literature. In Orthodox circles, especially in the Hasidic society, the old educational system was fiercely defended with no hint of compromise with the new emerging situation. Yet great changes occurred in Lithuanian religious society. In 1813 the great yeshiva *Etz Ḥayyim* was founded by Rabbi Ḥayyim Rabinowitz in Volozhin. This yeshiva had a set curriculum, a full-time staff and faculty, and the goal of producing the leaders and scholars for Jewry for the coming generations. It became known as the "mother of the yeshivot," and the yeshiva world today, though far removed from the original curriculum and perhaps even the goals of Volozhin, still claims descent and identity from it. The yeshiva in Volozhin at its maximum numbered close to four hundred students and there were rigid criteria for admittance. It was an elitist institution that successfully replicated itself in the world of Lithuanian Jewry throughout the period ending with the onset of World War II. Almost all of the great scholars and leaders of the rabbinic world in the nineteenth and early twentieth century were products of Volozhin. Volozhin had a seven-to-eight-year cycle of completing the entire Talmud with lectures being given by the faculty on every page of the Talmud. It also included intensive study of the Torah and the students were somehow well versed in Hebrew language and other Jewish studies.

The yeshiva system developed in Lithuania in the nineteenth century was an innovation in Jewish education. Other yeshivot copied it, though a more curtailed curriculum and an emphasis on the study and practice of *Musar* – the movement concentrating on piety of behavior and ethical dealings with others, founded by Rabbi Yisrael Lipkin of Salant – became the norm of the yeshiva movement worldwide. Some yeshivot such as Telshe had teachers' seminaries for both men and women affiliated with them. However, where the yeshiva movement in Lithuania was relatively small in numbers and elitist in its composition, today's yeshivot have very large numbers of students and, as a consequence, are much less elitist in terms of their student bodies' composition. This is undoubtedly true because of the fact that the society generally, and even Jewish society, is much more assimilationist and antireligious than was the case in nineteenth- and early twentieth-century Lithuania. Without a yeshiva education in the modern world a Jew is much less likely to be observant, marry Jewish and have Jewish grandchildren. The problem, however, is that the yeshivot still follow an elitist curriculum while providing education for the masses. Nevertheless, the amazing growth and popularity of the Lithuanian-type yeshiva movement in the late twentieth and early twenty-first centuries is a historical phenomenon of great and important note. It illustrates how the study of Torah, mainly for its own pure sake, is a recurring pattern throughout Jewish life and society in all eras.

The Hasidic world of eastern Europe stressed individual learning. There were no large yeshivot of note but rather those who devoted themselves to the study of Torah in their adult years did so at home or in the *shtiebel* – house of prayer and study, usually small in size – of their particular sect. It was not until the 1920s that a large yeshiva was founded in Poland. It was in Lublin and its head was Rabbi Me'ir Shapiro. The yeshiva had a rigorous entrance exam (two hundred folios of Talmud committed to memory and understanding) and numbered about two hundred students. It had a set curriculum, was much more Hasidic in nature and thought than the Lithuanian model, and served the elite of elite in Orthodox circles. It only functioned for a decade until destroyed – the yeshiva, not the building – by World War II. One of its former students told me that Rabbi Shapiro even wanted to insist on a uniform dress code in the institution but did not do so because of the differing nuances of Hasidic dress of its students. The yeshiva was housed in a magnificent building and provided for dormitory space and a functioning kitchen that served daily meals. All of this was an innovation in Polish Jewish Hasidic circles. Under the influence of the growing movement of Religious Zionism, a school of higher Jewish studies – *Taḥkamoni* – was established in Warsaw in the 1920s and its head was Rabbi Moshe Soloveitchik (who later left Poland and became the head of the yeshiva Rabbi Isaac Elchanan Theological Seminary, today part of Yeshiva University, in New York). This institution had a wider curriculum than the traditional yeshivot including history, language and philosophy. It too did not survive the onset of the war that began in 1939.

In Hungary and other places in central Europe three educational systems vied for influence and control of the Jewish community. The yeshiva world was represented by the institution located in Pressburg (today's Bratislava) in Slovakia. This yeshiva was founded in the 1800s by Rabbi Moshe Sofer (Ḥatam Sofer) and headed by his descendants again until World War II. It continues today in Jerusalem. It was Ashkenazic, non-Hasidic and produced most of the rabbinical leaders of the area for a century. Its curriculum and methods of study differed from those of the Lithuanian yeshivot. It placed a greater emphasis on the development of practical halakha and rabbinic training than did its Lithuanian counterparts, though the differences were more of nuance than of kind. There were also many secular school systems in Jewish Hungary that did include Jewish subjects such as Hebrew and Zionism but were, in the main, patterned after the non-Jewish schools of the time and place. The Hasidic influence grew in Hungary and Romania with many of the great Hasidic leaders of Galicia and Ukraine establishing their courts now in these countries. They steadfastly retained the traditional schooling methods and societies of their ancestors and contrasted sharply with the yeshiva system and certainly with the secular Jewish schools. Jewish Hungary was a land of extremes in the Jewish world – extremely rigorous and unbending in religious matters and outlooks and extremely liberal and even anti-religious in its secular institutions and values. A large proportion of Hungarian Jewry sent their children to the non-Jewish school system as did Polish Jewry. In the 1936 government census in Poland, seventy percent of Jewish children were registered in non-Jewish schools! The secularization of Jewish Europe in the period between the two terrible World Wars proceeded speedily and intensively. This certainly reflected itself in the field of traditional Jewish studies where two conflicting ideas arose as to how to stop this dangerous trend. One idea was to enter into new systems and reforms in the traditional methods and curriculums of Jewish education. The other stream felt the answer was to circle the wagons around the religious community and not to allow any changes in the traditional methods and curriculum of Jewish education. These two streams still vie for primacy in the religious Jewish world of the twenty-first century.

The great changes in Jewish education occurred in the United States in the twentieth century. In the early part of the century Jewish education was based on the afternoon Hebrew school. After a full day of studies in the American public-school system, the Jewish child was to attend a two- or three-hour study session four or five days a week. As can readily be imagined this type of situation did little to inspire love of Jewish studies among the students of these afternoon Hebrew schools. The Reform movement contented itself with a Sunday school program that also was of little value in instilling Jewish knowledge and values into its students. There were only a few large institutions of higher Torah study in America then. Located in New York were Yeshivot Rabbeinu Yitzḥak Elchanan, Mesivta Torah VoDaas, Rabbi Jacob Joseph School, Rabbinical Seminary of America, and Yeshivat Rabbeinu Chaim Berlin. In Chicago, Beis HaMidrash L'Torah/Hebrew Theological College serviced the Midwest part of the country while eventually Yeshivat Ner Israel established itself in Baltimore.

After World War II the yeshiva world of Europe was no longer.

The yeshivot in Israel were few and not very strongly populated. However, the arrival of a number of great, eastern European scholars who somehow escaped from the Germans signaled a new beginning for intensive Torah study in both Israel and the United States. Rabbi Yosef Shlomo Kahaneman established the Ponevezh yeshiva in Benei Berak, Israel, in the early 1940s and, later in the decade, Rabbi Eliezer Yehuda Finkel established Yeshivat Mir in Jerusalem. These institutions grew and expanded and had student bodies numbering in the thousands by the beginning of the twenty-first century. Their success in Israel was far greater than what it had even been in pre–World War II Lithuania. The same can be said for a number of yeshivot in Jerusalem, all flying the banner of Brisk and mainly under the direction of members of the Soloveitchik family. Whereas Brisk in Europe was marginal and small in the Lithuanian yeshiva world, today it is mainstream and quite large in numbers when all of its disparate branches are counted together.

In addition to these institutions many smaller Israeli yeshivot now began to grow and expand. Yeshivat Hebron was established in the 1920s, first in Jerusalem then in Hebron, and after the Hebron pogrom of 1929 rebuilt again in Jerusalem where it flourished anew. A network of Bnei Akiva yeshivot grew across the country. Many of them later became *yeshivot hesder,* combining army service with intensive Torah study. Yeshivat Mercaz HaRav, founded by Rabbi Abraham Isaac Kook in 1924, now became the flagship of Religious Zionist yeshivot in the country, though the yeshiva itself was not affiliated officially with any particular party or grouping. Universities in Israel offered wide-ranging intensive studies in Talmud, Bible, Jewish thought and history. Even the avowedly secular section of the population was provided with many programs and course offerings in Torah study that have become increasingly popular and influential. Great scholarly projects such as the Encyclopedia Talmudit and the Bar Ilan Responsa Project further intensified Torah study in the country. Literally hundreds of books on Torah and Talmud are published in Israel yearly and the new technology of the Internet, MP3s, DVDs, etc., has spread Torah far and wide to the masses of Israel. Torah study in Israel is far more popular and widespread today at the beginning of the twenty-first century than it was in many central and eastern European countries one hundred years earlier.

The same amazing revival of Torah study took place in the United States and Canada after World War II. Rabbi Eliyahu Meir Bloch reestablished Telshe Yeshiva in Cleveland, Ohio, in the 1940s, and his disciples founded and now administer two major yeshivot in Chicago and Riverdale, New York. Rabbi Aharon Kotler, the dynamic catalyst for much of the revival of Orthodox Jewish life in America and Israel, founded the great yeshiva in Lakewood, New Jersey, which today has many thousands of students engaged in fulltime Torah study. Rabbi Joseph B. Soloveitchik created a large cadre of followers and students, Torah scholars all, who occupy important rabbinic and educational roles in American Jewish life currently. Rabbi Avraham Kalmanowitz reestablished Yeshivat Mir in Brooklyn. There are many smaller, boutique-type yeshivot scattered throughout America and Canada. The state of New Jersey, for example, today contains more yeshivot than were extant in all of pre–World War II Lithuania! Intensive Torah study groups and classes for lay people and professionals exist in every Jewish community, large or small, throughout North America. Rabbi Meir Shapiro founded the Daf Yomi program – a daily study of one folio of the Talmud, completing the entire Talmudic cycle every seven and a half years – in 1923. Today there are probably more participants in this daily Torah study program than ever before. Mesorah Publications (Artscroll) and other publishers have made a great library of basic Jewish books – Bible, Mishna, Talmud, Midrash, Rashi, Ramban, etc. – available to the wider English-speaking public, thus further encouraging and enhancing Torah study.

The renaissance of Torah study over the past sixty years throughout the Jewish world, proves that the pattern of Torah rejuvenation after periods of apparent decline remains constant in Jewish life. The rabbis of the Talmud stated that the "Torah always returns to its original home." That home is Jewish society and the Jewish people. Torah is not merely an intellectual subject for Jews. It is an object of love and affection and it is the oxygen of Jewish life. A great sage once remarked that when we pray we speak to God. When we study Torah, God, as it were, speaks to us.

Chapter Four

Groupings and Movements

All organized faiths and religions have experienced the pattern of different and often opposing groupings developing within their midst. Schisms, violence, and even protracted decades-long wars between these internal groupings have beset both Christianity and Islam and all of the pagan Eastern faiths over their history. There seems to be an innate drive within members of all faiths to somehow attempt to improve, qualify or radically change past traditions or deeply held tenets of one's own faith in light of what is perceived as changing times, advanced technology and altered mores of society. And since we are dealing with faith issues, passions naturally run high and self-righteousness and exclusivity of the correctness of one's position rule the roost. Judaism and Jewish history also conform to this pattern of different groupings arising within the same faith-based community. Though the violence between the Jewish groups has toned down over the ages, the emotional contests and bitter disagreements have not diminished. The contest between different groupings within Jewish life over the ages is a recurrent feature of the story of the Jewish people.

Even though unity of purpose and loyalty of one Jew to another has always appeared as a desirable and imperative goal in Jewish life, the reality of Jewish history reveals a people of many different groupings and only rare instances of so-called Jewish societal unity. The Jewish nation was founded by twelve distinct and differing tribes, often in conflict with one another. Even in the slavery of Egypt not all Jews were treated equally, and amongst the Jews themselves there were differences between the tribes – the tribe of Levi was excused from hard labor, for instance. It was only at Mount Sinai that Jewish unity was achieved in the acceptance of the Torah by all of Israel. But this unity was not long lasting. It was in the nature of the tribes that each group looked after its self interest at the expense of the good of the whole. Thus the tribes of Reuben, Gad and part of Menashe broke away and settled east of the Jordan and did not live with the other tribes west of the Jordan in the Holy Land proper. The Torah's own separation of the tribe of Levi from the other tribes of Israel inexorably created a priestly and Levite grouping that eventually was not only a religious order but a social and political faction and power base as well. The book of Judges reveals to us the fragmentation of Jewish society after the death of Joshua and again how each of the tribes pursued their local good and welfare and did not act in concert with the other tribes. During the reigns of the prophet Samuel and Kings Saul, David and Solomon, the unity of the nation and its territorial integrity was restored. But this century of apparent unity disintegrated and after the death of Solomon, the Jewish people and its national state broke up into two differing and oftentimes warring groups – Israel (the ten tribes) in the north, and Judah (the tribes of Judah and Benjamin) in the south. Eventually the northern kingdom of Israel, having adopted idolatry as its faith in partnership somehow with Judaism, disappeared and many, though not all of its citizens were reabsorbed into the kingdom of Judah through the efforts of the prophet Jeremiah. But the pattern of groupings, divisions and break-offs in Jewish society was by now well established. It will continue throughout all of Jewish history.

Not all of the groupings and divisions within the people of Israel were caused internally. In First Temple times a large group of non-Jews were brought into the country from the Greek islands and settled in the area of Shomron/Samaria, north of Jerusalem. Afflicted by a large number of attacks from lions, they converted en masse to Judaism believing that the God of the country would protect them. This group existed and played a significant role in Jewish society – for good or for better – for almost a millennium. Uncertain of the true convictions of their conversion, the rabbis debated on whether the Samaritans were truly Jewish or not. When Ezra returned to Jerusalem with tens of thousands of Jews from the Babylonian exile, the Samaritans opposed him and the new Jewish settlements, as well as interfering with the attempts to build the Second Temple. Nevertheless they were not excluded from Jewish society at the time. However, when vestiges of paganism were still apparent in their society and worship centuries later – even though the Samaritans still upheld many important Jewish ritual practices stringently – the rabbis ruled this group not to be Jewish. The Samaritans separated themselves from Jewish society and are today a very small group living in Nablus in the land of Israel. Though not ever formally adopting Islam, they have nevertheless been heavily influenced by the surrounding Muslim society and are as inimical to Judaism and Jews as ever.

In the third century before the Common Era, under the influence of the Greek culture that then penetrated the land of Israel, a number of priests created a group called the *Tzedokim*/Sadducees. Originally a creation of an internal personal dispute over the succession to the office of the High Priest, the group soon took on a new theological bent. It denied the heavenly origin and authority of the Oral Law, attempted to deal with the Bible in a literal fashion, and rejected the rulings of the rabbinic leaders of Israel. It was heavily influenced by the glittering Greek culture of the time and from its midst eventually sprang a grouping of Jews – the Hellenists – who were determined to impose Greek beliefs, culture and worship on the Jewish people. The Sadducees were a powerful group for centuries and at certain times even controlled the Sanhedrin and the office of the High Priest. They represented the upper class of Jewish society and were wealthy and well connected to the Greek and later Roman authorities that ruled in the land of Israel during Second Temple times. Because of their connection to the Hellenists, the Sadducees lost temporary favor amongst the people of Israel during early Hasmonean times. However under the rule of the Hasmonean king, Alexander Yannai, they regained power. A second group, made up of rabbis, became known as *Perushim*/Pharisees. They opposed the Sadducees vigorously and upheld the centrality and divinity of the Oral Law of Sinai tenaciously. A civil war between the Pharisees and the Sadducees erupted with thousands of Jews killed and maimed in the ensuing battles. Persecuted unmercifully by Alexander Yannai, the Pharisees nevertheless later regrouped and regained power under the rule of his successor, Queen Shlomtziyon. The struggle between the Pharisees and the Sadducees continued throughout Second Temple times, though no longer in outright violent military battles, and many rabbinic ordinances and customs that were then instituted to combat the Sadducees are still present in Jewish daily life in our time.

A third grouping, small but eventually of some importance, came into being in Second Temple times. This group, the Essenes, practiced celibacy, excessive purification rituals, lived in the desert as hermits and promoted imminent messianic ideas and predictions. They held the Pharisees and the Sadducees in equal contempt and created a faith of immersions in water for purification and apocalyptic visions. It is from this group that the early Christians sprang and many of their practices remain in Christianity until today. Being celibate the group had to rely on outside conversions to its cause. The Essenes remained very small in number but they were the precursor of the worldwide religion of Christianity that came from their beliefs and society. The early Christians saw themselves as Jews and it was not until Paul at the end of the first century of the Common Era that the split between Christianity and Judaism became formal and irrevocable. Just as the rabbis had fought the Sadducees so did they struggle against the new faith that emanated from Jewish society. A special blessing was added to the thrice-daily prayers of Jews to guarantee that the Christian should realize that he was not part of the Jewish people. It was apparently a mutual de facto understanding between both camps that the Jews and the Christians would be delineated and separated and that this group of Jews would go its own way outside of Jewish society and life. From all of the struggles between the different groupings that arose during Second Temple times it was the Pharisees, the rabbinic group, that emerged triumphant, and with its continuing institution of the Oral Law of Sinai as being binding and decisive in all matters of Jewish law and life, defined normative Judaism for the following millennia. However, the bitter divisions within

Jewish society – aside from the groups already mentioned there were also extreme nationalist groupings who would rather die than to continue living under Roman rule, as well as roving gangs of outlaw thugs who preyed on innocent citizens – led to the eventual breakdown of law and order, then to rebellion against Rome and finally to the destruction of the Second Temple and the beginning of the long exile of Israel from its holy homeland.

Not all of the groupings that occurred in Jewish society during Second Temple times were negative. Within the society of the Pharisees itself there arose different groups and factions. The most noteworthy were the schools of Shammai and Hillel. These groups had different methodologies of study and different outlooks on life and Jewish value systems. The school of Hillel was more inclusive and numerous; the school of Shammai was more elitist and brilliant. Though the two schools were very different in character and viewpoint, they both subscribed to the supremacy of the Oral Law of Sinai and accepted each other on a tolerant and even cooperative basis. They married within each other's families and held that the Torah opinions expressed by each of the schools were "the words of the living God." Judaism has always thrived on differing opinions and even disparate social and ritual customs. The only caveat to this is that the framework of belief of Judaism – the divinity of the Written Torah and the authority of the Oral Law of Sinai – remain inviolate. The schools of Shammai and Hillel disagreed on 312 issues of Jewish law. Though they were certainly different, their differences were not only acceptable to all, but were considered to be a positive force in Jewish society. The pattern of this tension between groupings that were positive in Jewish life and those that were negative would repeat itself throughout Jewish history.

The destruction of the Second Temple and the resultant reign of terror by the Roman occupiers that followed, especially after the failure of the Bar Kokhba rebellion, served to minimize the rise of different groupings within the Jewish people for the next few centuries. The center of Jewish life was transferred to Babylonia where for almost a millennium it was the focus of Jewish learning and Torah study. The Babylonian Jewish community was organized on a system of parallel power. The heads of the famous yeshivot – the Geonim – were the spiritual and religious leaders of the people while the *Reish Galuta*/Exilarch was the head of the temporal matters of the community. This arrangement continued even when the Muslims took over power in the late seventh century and established the caliphate in Baghdad. As can readily be imagined there were periodic disputes and frictions between the *Reish Galuta* and the Geonim over where the power of each encroached on the other but there were no particular groupings or long-lasting divisions in Jewish society resulting from this continuing issue. However, in the eighth century there was a contest between brothers for the post of the *Reish Galuta* and the loser complained to the governmental authorities. In turn, he was accused of undermining the Jewish faith and community and condemned to death by the Muslim ruler of the country. He defended himself by saying that he was not undermining traditional Judaism but rather he represented a different religion than rabbinic Judaism. He was named Annan and the Jews who followed his lead were called Karaites. In spite of Annan's claims to the sultan, the Karaites saw themselves as being Jews and most Jewish halakhic authorities accepted them as such, albeit with some reservations and restrictions. Karaism adopted much of the program and theories of the defunct Sadducees and took on a literal interpretation of the Torah without the complementary understandings of the Oral Law of Sinai. The Karaites enjoyed originally sizable popularity but after a number of centuries they declined in numbers and influence as rabbinic Judaism and the Oral Law of Sinai once again triumphed over its detractors. Thus, the pattern of periodic rebellion against rabbinic Judaism and the authority of the Oral Law of Sinai as interpreted by the rabbinic leaders of Israel over the ages continued. This pattern of denial of the efficacy of the Oral Law of Sinai will take on different names of groupings over the ages of Jewish history, but a departure from Jewish tradition by any name still remains a departure from Jewish tradition. Karaism is only one of the names of these types of groupings that periodically create for themselves a new brand of Judaism to fit their newly imagined ideals or personal wishes.

A major difference in groupings occurred toward the end of the period of the Geonim approximately in the ninth century. Jews living in North Africa and under the rule and influence of expanding Muslim power and civilization began to move with the Muslims across the

Straits of Gibraltar into the Iberian Peninsula. These Jews originated from Babylonia and the land of Israel, and a number of the Babylonian Geonim found their way to North Africa and were of great influence upon the local communities in which they resided. These North African and Spanish Jews developed their own customs and way of life, enjoying for a number of centuries the tolerance of the civilized Muslim rulers of the time. This was the Golden Age of Spanish Jewry. These Jews, known collectively as Sephardim – *Sefarad* was the traditional name in Hebrew for Spain – constituted in the early Middle Ages the majority of Jews in the world. The center of Torah learning moved from Babylonia, whose Jewish power and community began to decline because of changing demographic and economic circumstances, to North Africa and Spain. The Spanish Jews were poets, astronomers, philosophers, physicians, linguists, courtiers, diplomats and even military leaders. They developed a rich culture of Jewish life that included all types of professions, trades and scholars. Their greatness in Torah, represented by such scholars as Rabbi Yitzḥak Alfasi, Rabbi Moshe ben Maimon, Rabbi Yosef ibn MiGash, Rabbi Moshe ben Naḥman, Rabbi Shlomo ben Aderet, Rabbi Yona Gerondi, Rabbi Yom Tov ibn Ashbili and Rabbi Nissim ben Reuven, was unquestioned. Their influence in the entire Jewish world extended over the Middle East and especially in Egypt and later in Babylonia itself. With the exception of a number of decades, they lived comfortably among the Muslims. However when the Christian reconquest of Spain in the thirteenth century gained steam, the Jewish situation changed radically.

The Jews were expelled from Spain in 1492. The Sephardim spread over all of Europe, especially to the Netherlands and the Mediterranean basin and the Near East. The Jews of Iraq, Iran and Yemen were also reckoned as Sephardim though that is not at all accurate. Today they are allied with the Sephardic grouping in the eyes of most Jews though they are really the "communities of the East" – a separate grouping unto itself. Most Sephardim returned to live in Muslim lands and though no "Golden Age" recurred they generally did not suffer the ravages that Christian Europe perpetrated on their Ashkenazic brothers. The Sephardim lived quite separate from the other Jewish groupings in the world. They did not experience the Crusades, Reformation, the Renaissance, Enlightenment, Reform, the rise of Hasidism or *Musar* or the Lithuanian yeshiva movement, political Zionism and to a large extent (with the exception of the Balkans) the Holocaust. They had a different background and view of life than the Ashkenazim. Thus the shock of their sudden forced reunification with other groupings of Jews when they came to Israel in the 1950s undermined their communities greatly. Torn from their roots and traditions, their family structures and behavior demeaned by those who "knew better what was really good for them," and confused by the new environment that they now lived in, many of the Sephardim felt rootless, discriminated against, and many more lost their self-respect and loyalty to Jewish values. This pattern was reversed later beginning in the 1970s when people such as Rabbi Ovadya Yosef and others restored self- pride to the Sephardic community, and the political party *Shas* gave this community political and social clout. Rabbi Yosef's motto for Sephardic rebirth and regeneration was "to return the crown to its former self." The reemergence of Sephardic Jewry as a powerful and influential force in Jewish life the world over has added great vitality and resources to the Jewish world as a whole.

The other great grouping that arose in the very early Middle Ages was the Ashkenazim. Babylonian Jews in the ninth and tenth centuries migrated through the Balkans and eventually reached France and the Rhineland. There were Jewish communities in those areas during the period of Roman rule. The founding strength of the community was based on the great personality of Rabbeinu Gershom, known as the "Light of the Exile." In the tenth century, Rabbeinu Gershom established on a permanent basis a great yeshiva in Mainz. However, the Ashkenazic community at that time, concentrated in the Ile de France and the Rhineland, was quite small in number, probably no more than a few hundred families. Rabbeinu Gershom convened the leaders of that community and a number of important decrees were adopted which have remained in force until today. Primary amongst those decrees was (1) a prohibition against polygamy; (2) women could not be divorced against their consent; (3) levirate marriages were not to be consummated; and (4) letters addressed to others were not to be opened by anyone except the addressee. Many other decrees and laws and customs from that time and place became the basis of the society of the Ashkenazim in the Middle Ages and later. The Ashkenazic community developed over the next century – until the destruction of the Jewish communities in the Rhineland in the First Crusade in 1096 – especially under the leadership of Rabbi Shlomo Yitzḥaki (Rashi) of Troyes (1040–1105) and his students and family. A great proportion of Ashkenazic Jewry can trace some of their ancestry back to Rashi and his family. Rashi's great commentaries to the Bible and Talmud, and those of his students and descendants, the Tosafists, remain the standby and standout texts of Jewish learning generally, and Talmudic scholarship particularly, until today. Through these texts, the Ashkenazic community gained great influence over their Sephardic brethren as well.

Unlike the Sephardim, the Ashkenazim did not engage in philosophy, poetry, the arts and non-Jewish communal and political affairs to any great degree. They lived a Talmudical existence and their main concentration was on Torah study. Hated and despised, persecuted and oftentimes slaughtered by their Christian neighbors, they developed an insular and isolated way of life and were fiercely proud of their ethnic origins. They eventually moved eastwards and came to Poland in the fourteenth century and spread throughout Central and Eastern Europe as well. In spite of continuing persecution, discrimination and pogroms, the Ashkenazic community became the largest population of the Jewish people. However, the Ashkenazim, much more so than the Sephardim, would be wracked by inner divisions and bitter splits, some of which will soon be detailed in this chapter. The Holocaust of World War II destroyed the majority of Ashkenazic Jewry though much of the community has since been rebuilt and revitalized. To a great extent Ashkenazic Jewry, because of its numbers, experiences and social and national environments, has been the dominant force in Jewish history over the last five centuries. Ashkenazic Jewry itself is subdivided into many different sub-groupings and therefore like all major groupings in the Jewish world should not be viewed as being monolithic.

Other smaller groupings like Roma (Italian) Jews and Provencal Jews also existed for centuries. They were neither Ashkenazim nor Sephardim though naturally they were influenced by both of those large groupings. Italian Jewry was heavily influenced by Renaissance and its theories and mores. The Jews of Provence were a cockpit of controversy regarding the place of philosophy and secular studies in Jewish life and especially regarding some of the works of Maimonides. The oldest medical school in Europe in Montpelier was founded by Provencal Jews in the tenth and eleventh centuries. The Jews of Yemen, Bukhara and the Caucasus are also smaller groupings within the whole of the fabric of the Jewish people. The fact that the Jews were scattered over the entire face of the earth naturally created many small groupings and differences amongst Jews of different areas and climes. Nevertheless, it can be said that over the long history of the Jewish people it was the basic loyalty to Torah and tradition that bound disparate Jews together and created a sense of Jewish nationhood even in exile and difficult circumstances. The Jewish people was originally formed from twelve different tribes, and the ability to sustain a unique and mostly autonomous people formed of different tribes and groupings remained a staple of Jewish life throughout its long and varied history.

The eighteenth century in Europe brought about the formation of a number of large new groupings within the Jewish people. The previous century was wracked by the schism caused by the false messiah, Shabbetai Tzvi and his Polish successor Jacob Frank. But the Sabbateans – the followers of Shabbetai Tzvi – and the Frankists – the followers of Jacob Frank – were soon marginalized and no longer constituted a significant grouping within Jewish religious or social life. However, these groups of false messianists accomplished great harm during their few days of influence, weakening the authority of the rabbinic establishments in Europe and eventually undermining the faith in the advent of the miraculous messianic era. The spread of the ideas of the Enlightenment in the early eighteenth century signaled a new era for the Jews in Europe, especially for those in Germany and in central Europe. There were many positive things that the Enlightenment provided for European Jewry: a previously unknown degree of tolerance in Christian society; admittance to universities and, to a lesser degree, to the professions and arts; the removal of ghetto walls and Jewish isolation. But these were balanced and perhaps outweighed by the Enlightenment's negative traits from a Jewish perspective – its vehement anti-religion stance and its agnosticism toward the Bible and previously accepted social traditions and mores. The Enlightenment's doctrine of the separation of

Church from State would work well in the newly created United States of America but less well in France and in other European countries. There is no question that the eighteenth century witnessed the rise of ascendant secularism in Western civilization, a trend that continues to grow in our time centuries later. And Jewish society would not escape being almost swept away by this tidal social and philosophical trend.

The Jewish Enlightenment is usually ascribed in its beginnings to the singular personage of Moses Mendelssohn, a German Jew of the eighteenth century. Mendelssohn himself was an observant Jew and corresponded with many of the great rabbinic scholars of his time. However, his philosophy and view of the Bible was heavily influenced by critical Enlightenment attitudes toward the holiness and divinity of the Bible and the rational criticism and agnosticism toward traditional religious and folk beliefs, and thus his views and very personality were the source of continuing controversy over his place in the traditional Jewish world. A wave of conversions to Christianity began to sweep German Jews with the fall of the ghetto walls. Many Jews felt that conversion was the only way to really get ahead in the new environment of emancipation and enlightenment. Being Christian in the eighteenth and nineteenth century was the obvious ticket to the higher levels of European society and thus thousands of Jews converted, mostly originally insincerely, to Christianity to have their ticket punched. As previously mentioned, four of Mendelssohn's own children converted to Christianity, and all of his grandchildren, including the famous composer Felix Mendelssohn, were Christians. This sad state of his descendants weighed heavily against Mendelssohn himself in later generations in the eyes of the traditional Jewish community. Many have attempted to rehabilitate him but in the Orthodox Jewish world of today he has few defenders outside of academia.

As a result of the Enlightenment and the sudden large numbers of German and later Austrian Jews who now considered conversion to Christianity as a viable option for their advancement in life and society, a new movement, Reform, emerged. Reform despaired of Jewish existence in a modern Western society if Judaism remained in its traditional form, rituals and observances. In its haste to become accepted in German society, Reform renounced any attachment to the land of Israel,

Hebrew language and messianic hopes. It also eliminated most of the rituals of Judaism, its dietary laws and family purity restrictions. Sunday now substituted for the Sabbath and it placed great emphasis upon what it thought as being the moral values of Judaism. The church organ performed in its temples and all heads were by doctrine uncovered. It attempted to make Judaism a sort of "Jewish Christianity" emphasizing the surface similarities of the two faiths and glossing over any of the main stark differences of belief and traditions. It made Berlin its new Jerusalem and its followers became good Germans of the Mosaic persuasion. It made great headway in the cities of Germany but the smaller towns and villages of Germany were steadfastly traditional, rejecting Reform. The Reform movement had great influence and a large following in Germany, France, and the Austro-Hungarian empire. In the late 1840s it successfully transplanted itself to the United States where its program was even more radical than it had been in western Europe. Reform in America created the infrastructure of American Jewry, an infrastructure dedicated to achieving the full assimilation of Jews into American life and culture, oftentimes doctrinally and willingly at the expense of any meaningful commitment to even minimal Jewish beliefs and practices.

Reform was unsuccessful in exporting itself to eastern Europe, the heartland of Ashkenazic Jewry, or to the Sephardic world. Eventually its popularity in Germany itself waned as the plague of conversions to Christianity continued unabated. Its strength now grew in America where for over a century it laid claim to representing the proper American Jewish way of life. However, by the beginning of the twenty-first century it was declining in numbers and influence even there. Over the last half of the twentieth century, Reform in many ways turned more traditional, abandoning some of the radicalism of its earlier generations. However, it approved of patrilineal descent in defining Jewishness (Israeli Reform did not adopt this idea) and eventually became the haven for intermarried couples. It advocated all current liberal ideas of the time regarding same-sex unions and behavior, had women clergy and took true Jewish education very lightly. Very few present-day Reform Jews had ancestors who were themselves Reform. Most Reform Jews were descended from Orthodox Jewish households who had become acculturated and then assimilated. The pattern of initial great success followed by eventual decline that controlled the fate of the Sadducees and the Karaites seems to be repeating itself regarding the Reform movement.

However, eastern European Jewry did not escape the effects of Emancipation and the Enlightenment. In eastern Europe it reflected itself in the forming of the *Haskala*/Enlightenment movement. While Reform dealt with Jewish theology, *Haskala* originally dealt with culture and social mores. *Haskala* emphasized adaptability to modern ways, and the amalgamation of general studies and European cultures into Jewish schools and life. Eventually, *Haskala* convinced itself that the Jewish people could and would prosper and survive on the basis of its cultural heritage and not necessarily as a religion of obligations and ritual duties. It removed religious observances from public Jewish life. It substituted the humanist values of the Enlightenment (it repackaged them as "prophetic" Judaism) for core Jewish beliefs. Its slogan was "Be a Jew in your home but a regular human being in public." As appealing as that slogan may sound at first hearing, it led to the assimilation and conversion of hundreds of thousands of Jews who were unable to safely navigate that slippery slope. In many respects it created a schizophrenic personality, with a great deal of pangs of conscience and no shortage of self-hate as well. Karl Marx, Heinrich Heine and to a lesser extent Benjamin Disraeli are all examples of those who fell down that treacherous slope created by the Enlightenment and its rejection of religion and tradition. It also mistakenly maintained that the promotion of Jewish culture at the expense of religion, faith and Jewish observances would diminish if not completely eliminate anti-Semitism. This was probably the greatest example of the naivety of *Haskala* and its adherents. Neither Hitler, Stalin nor Arafat was duly impressed by the richness of thought, creativity and scholarship of the Jewish culturists.

The *Haskala* movement came in various forms. There was a Hebrew *Haskala* that attempted to revive the ancient holy language and make it the basic spoken and written language of Jews. Hebrew poetry, novels and newspapers abounded in the heyday of the Hebrew *Haskala* in the nineteenth century. The Hebrew *Haskala* eventually married political Zionism and found a new and firmly based home in the emerging secular Jewish society in the land of Israel. The Yiddish *Haskala* developed a wide ranging culture of literature and theatre as well.

It especially became associated with the rise of the Jewish labor unions and Socialist parties in eastern Europe and later in the United States. The Yiddish *Haskala* soon took on an anti-tradition form and eventually became almost atheistic in its outlook. The Yiddish *Haskala* also became associated with the Jewish Left – Socialism, Communism and other radical Marxist groups. The Bolsheviks who hijacked Russia in 1917 eliminated the remnants of the Hebrew *Haskala* completely. Peculiarly, at the onset of their power, they encouraged the Yiddish *Haskala*. However, Stalin's postwar anti-Semitic mania eliminated the Yiddish *Haskala* as well. Both the Hebrew and Yiddish *Haskala* developed their own school systems, which for decades successfully competed with the traditional *ḥeder* and yeshiva systems of traditional Jewry. For a time these school systems existed in American Jewish life too but within a century essentially disappeared from the American Jewish scene. There was also a Russian form of *Haskala* that based the future of eastern European Jewry on being accepted into Russian society via the adoption of Russian culture and language. This type of *Haskala* was openly assimilationist and eventually led to members of the then Jewish intelligentsia converting to Christianity to advance themselves in Russian society.

The *Haskala* movement, especially the Hebrew *Haskala*, influenced the traditional Jewish world in many ways but generally speaking it engendered almost universal opposition from all sections of the traditional world. Eventually the *Haskala* came to represent the beginning of the attempted total secularization of much of eastern European Jewry and was sensed to be basically anti-religious in its nature and goals. By the end of the nineteenth century the strength of the *Haskala* movement weakened, never having been able to achieve its goals of successfully assimilating Jews into Russian society, decreasing anti-Semitism or improving the day-to-day life of eastern European Jews. It was salvaged however from potential oblivion when it merged with political Zionism and much of its cultural program was adopted by the general Zionist movement. Culture became the watchword of the Zionist movement as well and, when combined with nationalism, it emerged a potent force in Jewish life in the twentieth century. This idea of Jewish culture alone as a fulcrum of continuing Jewish life proved unable to stem the tide of Jewish assimilation in America and is the subject of ongoing controversy and difficulty in modern-day Israel as well. The pattern of substituting other forms of content and ideals for Torah life and values is well known and clearly documented in Jewish history. In the long run of history's time clock, it always proves to be a failure.

In the eighteenth and nineteenth centuries new movements arose within the traditional Jewish world itself. These movements subscribed to Jewish tradition fully, recognized the divinity of the Torah and fulfilled the commandments and ritual demands of Jewish life. Nevertheless, they represented a departure from the behavior, mores and even the ideas of normative medieval Judaism, which until then held sway in Jewish existence. These movements were all products of Ashkenazic Jewry and to a great extent were a reaction to the advent of the Enlightenment and its effect on European Jewry. The largest, most successful and longest lasting movement was that of Hasidism. Originating in the 1730s in Volhynia, its leader was the mysterious and charismatic Rabbi Yisrael Ba'al Shem Tov. The movement laid greater emphasis on prayer, charity, social bonds, joy of life and service, songs and stories and the importance of the Tzaddik/Rebbe/Holy Leader in Judaism than it originally did on Torah scholarship itself and the authority of the Torah scholar. None of the ideas or beliefs of Hasidism were new – they existed for many centuries before Rabbi Yisrael Ba'al Shem Tov. It was the emphasis upon these ideas and the primacy now attached to them over other goals and norms that were new and even unprecedented. It was a movement for the masses and shunned the elitism of the then established Torah and communal lay authorities. It was heavily kabbalistic (essentially Lurianic Kabbala) in thought and outlook and dealt deeply with mysticism, spirituality and messianism. Contrary to previous generations, it publicized all of these kabbalistic and mystical ideas, making them the property of the masses that perhaps were unable to assess and understand them correctly. It had elements of social and religious radicalism in it and was opposed strongly by the leading rabbis of the time, some of whom subjected it to vehement bans and excommunication. Nevertheless, the movement grew and prospered, modified its behavior and theology and became part of the mainstream of normative Jewish life in eastern and even central Europe. A century after its founding it had enlisted a majority of eastern European Jews in its ranks and was the main opponent of *Haskala* and the secularization of Jewish society in the nineteenth century. Since Hasidism was basically kabbalistically oriented and adopted a supernatural view of life and events, it naturally had no room for the ideas and programs of super-rational *Haskala* within its worldview. Hasidism strongly undermined the authority of the established rabbinate, and the institution of the Tzaddik/Rebbe/Holy Man eclipsed the exalted position of the communal rabbis of the time and later as well. The Hasidic movement itself, by its very nature, splintered into hundreds of sub-groups, some large and powerful and others small and very localized, and there was fierce competition and disputes – sometimes even violence – between these sub-groupings. The Hasidic movement spawned many great and holy leaders whose influence was not limited to their group or location or time. The *Haskala* attacked and ridiculed Hasidism unmercifully and saw it as its main enemy for dominance in the then Ashkenazic Jewish society. Hasidism, though suffering from attrition in its ranks due to secularization and the rising popularity of the promises and programs of the utopian idealism of the Left amongst Jewish youth, nevertheless stood its ground and eventually prevailed and prospered. Every action begets a reaction. It is no exaggeration to say that the advent of *Haskala* and its ideas forced the response that the rising of the Hasidic movement exemplified.

Another nineteenth-century grouping arose in Lithuania, the bastion of anti-Hasidic thought and society. Founded in the 1840s by the charismatic genius, Rabbi Yisrael Lipkin of Salant, this movement of *Musar*/Jewish Ethics attempted to change Jewish life-style and correct many of the failings of the traditional society of the time. Rabbi Lipkin's pithy comment summed up its purpose nicely: "Reform came to change Judaism; *Musar* comes to change Jews!" Originally envisaged by its founder as a mass movement that would raise the consciousness and behavior of the ordinary lay person, it soon became almost the exclusive province of the Lithuanian yeshivot of the time. Thus the movement was essentially elitist, restricted to perhaps a few thousand adherents. Nevertheless it had great influence in the Jewish world because the rabbinic and yeshiva leaders of the late nineteenth and most of the twentieth century in Europe, America and the land of Israel were all products and graduates of the Lithuanian yeshiva world that emphasized *Musar* in Jewish life and studies. Famous classics of Jewish thought and ethics, which were rarely read or studied (such as the eighteenth-century *Mesilat Yesharim* by Rabbi Moshe Ḥayyim Luzatto and the thirteenth-century *Darkhei Teshuva* by Rabbeinu Yona Gerondi among others), now became staples of study in the yeshiva world. There was fierce opposition to the *Musar* movement at its onset with many leading rabbinic authorities objecting to the study of *Musar* as somehow diminishing the study of Talmud itself in the yeshivot. Rabbi Lipkin's famous retort to this accusation is encompassed in an answer that he gave to someone who asked him: "Rabbi, I have only ten minutes a day to study Torah. Should I study Talmud or *Musar*?" Rabbi Lipkin coolly replied: "Study *Musar*. You will then soon realize that you actually have more than ten minutes a day to study Torah." By the beginning of the twentieth century the opposition to *Musar* waned. However, the Holocaust destroyed most of the great luminaries of *Musar*; they proved to be irreplaceable and thus, by the end of the century, it had lost its previous popularity and vitality even in the yeshivot that still subscribed to its heritage and curriculum.

Musar can be seen as a reaction of the Torah world to some of the valid criticisms of *Haskala* to the mores of Jewish society in nineteenth-century Russia. It attempted to rectify obvious social imbalances, protect the defenseless and the poor, restore honesty to the marketplace, exalt prayer and the performance of ritual observances and create greater social harmony. Like Hasidism, the *Musar* movement also had various sub-groupings within it. *Musar* declined as a movement because of its inability in the latter half of the twentieth century to prove itself truly relevant to a society of affluence and independence. The rabbis of the Talmud noted that Judaism and the Jews do better, spiritually and morally speaking, in times of poverty rather than in times of wealth. This certainly was true of the *Musar* movement. Although it outlasted *Haskala* in Lithuania and certainly in its yeshivot, by the beginning of the twenty-first century, the non-Hasidic "Lithuanian" traditional world was much closer in thought and behavior to the Hasidic world than to any strong feelings of heritage from *Musar*. The *Musar* movement never spread to the Hasidic or Sephardic societies and remained primarily a Lithuanian yeshiva-oriented movement. Still, the appearance and existence of the *Musar* movement is itself a prime example of the pattern of the continuing attempts toward spiritual renewal and moral cleansing that repeats itself throughout Jewish history.

Another movement arose in nineteenth-century Germany that dealt with the pressures that the Enlightenment forced upon the traditional Jewish society. This movement somehow came to be called Neo-Orthodoxy. It advocated strict observance of all Jewish rituals, norms and customs coupled with an intensive secular education and the entry of Orthodox Jews into all available professions and commerce of the general society. I have previously discussed the differing views of Rabbi Azriel Hildesheimer and Samson Raphael Hirsch as to the structure of this movement – whether it was to be a synthesis of Jewish and secular knowledge or merely the acquisition of two different systems of knowledge and information. Rabbi Hirsch called it *Torah im Derekh Eretz*. Neo-Orthodoxy created the "perfect" German Jew. Unlike Reform, these Jews were Jewish in the full sense of the traditional meaning of the word while at the same time remaining German to the core. In Germany this proved to be the strongest refutation of Reform's assimilationist policies, creating a "modern" Jew without compromising Jewish faith and practice. Both Rabbis Hirsch and Hildesheimer thought that this model, if adopted in eastern European Jewish society, would stem the tide of secularization and the negative influences of *Haskala*. In effect, they believed that this German model could and should be replicated everywhere in the Jewish world and that this was the best and only method to combat the new pressures that the Enlightenment, modernism, secularization and urbanization were creating in Jewish society. However, the rabbis of eastern European Jewry were of the opinion that what worked for Germany and its Jews had no place in eastern Europe. Neo-Orthodoxy never spread east successfully. Nevertheless, it did, like Reform, successfully export itself to the United States where it eventually evolved into Modern Orthodoxy or today's Centrist Orthodoxy. Yeshiva University, Young Israel, Bar-Ilan University, Touro College and other such institutions and organizations in the Jewish world are examples of this movement's influence and direction. Even some mainstream yeshivot in America, officially or unofficially, allow their students to attend secular college programs outside of the all-day programs of the yeshiva itself. The pattern of this type of willing and voluntary adjustment to the larger society that had occurred in Spain and parts of the Middle East in the Middle Ages was thus now repeated in Germany and later in the United States, Israel and the rest of the Western world. And the opposition to this type of societal adjustment that existed in the Middle Ages, especially in the Ashkenazic world, also again repeated itself in the modern era, originally in Eastern Europe, but later in Israel, America and all other places in the Jewish world as well. Even today, much of the Hasidic and yeshiva worlds reject any form of advanced secular education for their adherents. Therefore the pattern of this long standing disagreement regarding the place of secular education and all that it entails and leads to in traditional Jewish society – attempted full integration but not assimilation into the general society – still continues in all of its doctrinally inspired vehemence in today's Jewish world. There have been many attempts to bridge this difference, and on a personal level much success has been achieved in doing so, but on an organizational and ideological level no satisfactory middle ground has yet emerged to general satisfaction.

In the United States, in addition to the movements of Reform, Neo-Orthodoxy and traditional Orthodoxy, secularism, Marxism and the Left that all immigrated to the "golden land," there arose another movement that fashioned itself "Conservative" Judaism. This movement, which was founded at the beginning of the twentieth century with Dr. Solomon Schechter of Cairo Geniza fame as the head of its Jewish Theological Seminary, felt that Judaism had to adjust to American life and that therefore, certain compromises in Jewish observance and ritual were inevitable if American Jews were to remain Jewish. It saw its role as "conserving" as much of tradition as possible under the changing Jewish environment of American life. The Jewish Theological Seminary, until the 1960s, had a faculty composed mainly of Orthodox Jewish scholars of note who attempted to hold on to the traditions of Jewish European life in spite of the more liberal theology that guided its pulpit rabbis and congregants in the field. With the passing of these scholars, the Seminary itself by the end of the century became a bastion of liberalism on many social and halakhic issues in Jewish society and thus further distanced itself from its original Orthodox roots. Never intending to be as extreme as Reform in its theology and practice, Conservative Judaism nevertheless shed most of its traditional raiment and eventually, over a century, became a slightly less radical and paler imitation of Reform. Conservative Judaism remained fundamentally an American phenomenon and its attempts to become a worldwide movement were mainly unsuccessful. It could not maintain itself on the slippery slope that it had originally climbed and staked out for itself, and declined substantially in the latter decades of the twentieth century, a decline that continues now in the twenty-first century as well. It is an example of movements that arose in Jewish history and ostensibly served a purpose in the short run but disappeared eventually, unable to successfully survive in the long run.

The movements that concerned themselves with the land of Israel will be discussed in Chapter Six.

The wry remark "one Jew, two synagogues," certainly seems to hold with the active and continuing pattern of multiplicity of Jewish groupings and movements that mark the Jewish scene. As mentioned above, we began our nationhood as twelve separate tribes, often warring with one another, and this pattern has continued throughout our history. Like all trends and characteristics in life, it has had its advantages and its liabilities. We should all hope for a sense of unity in Jewish life and be wise enough never to expect or even desire conformity. It is the nuance of difference that revitalizes the eternal people and allows it to constantly refresh and renew itself. Those groupings and movements whose basic allegiances lie in Torah study, observance and values have been shown to be able to withstand the test of time and vicissitude. Those groupings and movements that abandoned Jewish tradition eventually, some quickly, some over many centuries, fell by the wayside. This has also been an inexorable pattern in the story of the Jewish people.

Chapter Five

Women

I hesitate to write this chapter for a variety of reasons. Many women have told me in my rabbinic career that men lecturing or writing about women's issues is a sure loser from the outset. I only defend myself to that charge by stating that since I am descended from a long line of women, I am brave enough to undertake this challenge.

Perhaps no greater change has occurred in internal Jewish life over the last century than the changing role of women in Jewish family, social and communal life. In many families it is now the woman who is the breadwinner of the house, something that was a rarity in past Jewish generations. We have recorded instances of eastern European women in the nineteenth century, though not earlier, operating businesses while their husbands spent their time almost exclusively in Torah study and/or communal service and endeavors. And even in those cases such as that of Rabbi Yisrael Me'ir Kagan (Ḥafetz Ḥayyim) and the store operated by his wife, the woman was not the primary breadwinner. The store was reduced to being a secondary source of income with the books of Rabbi Kagan becoming the main generator of family income as attested to in the biography of Rabbi Kagan by his son, Rabbi Aryeh Leib Poupko.

Jewish women today enjoy wide access to all professions and

spheres of the modern world. In certain circles women are well known for Torah scholarship and teach and lecture regularly on Torah subjects. There are women's seminaries and colleges. Nechama Leibowitz, among others, has gained a position of insight through her commentary on the Torah itself, entirely based on knowledge and exposition of rabbinic, traditional source material. Pious, observant Jewish women find themselves in the workplace as computer specialists, actuaries, physicians, graphic artists, publishers, therapists, entrepreneurs, teachers, lawyers, administrators and many other fields outside the home activity. It has not always been this way, though a pattern regarding the place of women in Jewish life and history can be traced.

I further definitely hesitate to make any comments about the great women figures that appear in the Bible. No people in our age can truly appreciate and comment upon the qualities and character of the biblical personages except for the glimpses into their lives and personalities afforded us by Midrash and Talmud and the great commentators of the ages. Nevertheless, we do have a binding rabbinic rule that the words of the Bible are to be understood in their simple meaning as well. Thus it is worthwhile to note that there were women prophets, judges, teachers and leaders amongst the Jewish people in biblical times. Sarah, Rebecca, Leah, Rachel, Tamar, Miriam, Yokheved, Tzippora, Seraḥ, Devora, Raḥav, Yael, Ḥulda, are only some of the examples that come to mind. It is obvious that these extraordinary women played a leading role in the spiritual, physical and national development of the Jewish people for centuries on end. In a general world society of feminine exploitation and abuse, of illiteracy and abject servitude, women in Jewish life were seemingly granted opportunity for personal and communal advancement and leadership roles. There is no way for us to know whether such a general pattern of women's participation in national and spiritual Jewish life was a widespread condition in biblical times or whether it was only these exceptional personalities mentioned here that were so involved. When the Torah was granted to Israel on Mount Sinai, the Lord demanded, so to speak, that Moses mobilize not only the men of Israel but the Jewish women (*Beit Yaakov*) as well for this cause – the acceptance of this eternal mission of Godliness and education and pious personal example. Great commentators have pointed out that the Torah was and is a fiery religion and study – *esh dat.* Men may have concentrated on the study part of Torah, especially the Oral Law, but the fire of faith and Torah was passed on by the women of Israel. The Talmud relates to us that the women of Israel refused to contribute their jewelry to the building of the Golden Calf and did not participate in the numerous rebellions against Moshe and God in the desert of Sinai. According to some rabbinic opinion the women of Israel entered the Holy Land with Joshua and were not subjected to the decree that eliminated the generation that left Egypt from entry into the land of Israel. Thus from the beginnings of our history the presence of women in educational and leadership roles was well established.

Women played a malevolent role in biblical Jewish life as well. Atalia and Jezebel are two prime examples of such women. Powerful queens, both of the northern kingdom of the ten tribes of Israel and Judah, as well as of outside countries, heavily influenced Jewish life in biblical times. King Solomon in Proverbs and in Ecclesiastes extols the magnificent qualities of women and the dire consequences that can befall those who are in the clutches of evil females. Again, neither I nor anyone else can peer into that biblical society, a time when the *Shekhina* – God's holy spirit, so to speak – was palpably present in Jewish society and in its holy Temple in Jerusalem, and make any definitive judgments or conclusions. Nevertheless, it does seem obvious from a simple reading of the texts that women played a prominent public role in all aspects of that society. Perhaps this is because the Jews were able to build a particularly independent society, albeit not completely free from pagan influences and practices, with abundant powers of prophecy present as a guide to how that society should function and prosper. In such a society of Jewish political independence, women were able to play an important role in the leadership and influence of the country.

In Second Temple times women continued to be of influence and even power. The strength of the Pharisees – the rabbis of the Mishna who disseminated and upheld the Oral Law of Sinai – was enhanced by the coming to power of Queen Shlomtziyon (Salome Alexandra) after the death of her violently anti-Pharisee husband Alexander Yannai. She was the sister of the *tanna* Shimon ben Shetaḥ, and he was appointed by her to serve as what we may call the prime minister of the country.

Under her guidance and his initiative, a school system for all Jewish children was established, as was a legitimate Sanhedrin. In the Mishna and Talmud, women of great substance and scholarship appear. Among them are Beruria, the wife of Rabbi Me'ir; "Ima," the mother of Rav; and Yalta, the wife of Rav Naḥman. Again, whether these women represent the then norm of educated women, especially of those who were daughters and wives of Torah scholars, or whether they were merely the exceptions to the rule of society where women were not educated, cannot be easily ascertained. In any event, it is interesting that the Talmud quotes their opinions and speaks of them respectfully. In Roman times, and in Babylonia as well, women of the non-Jewish aristocracy were well educated, powerful and most influential. The Talmud records for us powerful non-Jewish women, such as Queen Hilni (Helena of Adiabene), who had direct contact with the rabbis and were accorded great respect by them. In the Talmud we find two opinions as to the necessity and efficacy of teaching Torah to women: one positive and one negative. In later times both opinions would be followed depending upon location, environment and convention. It is from this that the differing patterns of Jewish life vis-à-vis women emanated and ebbed and flowed throughout the ages.

Yet in all times modesty of dress and behavior between men and women was stressed as a Jewish value and virtue, a halakhic norm. Beruria's lectures in Torah were delivered from a screened podium. The Talmud records the separation of seating at funerals and certainly at other occasions. At the great annual celebration on the holiday of Sukkot marking the libation of water on the Temple's altar, a special balcony was built for the women to separate them from the men so that the celebration would not cross the boundaries of modesty and probity. Lewdness in speech and behavior was abhorred and forbidden. But on the other hand, the rabbis of the Talmud went to great lengths to protect the honor, financial security and social status of women. The rise of early Christianity, which was in many ways a promotion of celibate behavior and other eventually anti-women attitudes and the dissolute behavior norms of the dissolving Roman Empire, only intensified the rabbis' efforts to help the status of women in Jewish society. A great deal of legal and practical effort was expended in laws regarding divorce, *agunot* (wives whose husbands had disappeared and their death could not be officially validated), recalcitrant husbands who would not grant their wives a proper and timely divorce, and other matters of domestic relations. Over the ages, all of these problems – unfortunately common to human nature and society – continued to exist in the Jewish world in varying intensity and frequency. But the basic pattern of halakhic attitude and ruling was already set millennia ago, though it has been tweaked regularly in different generations and circumstances.

The rise of Islam in the seventh century and the beginnings of the breakdown of the hegemony of the Babylonian scholars over Jewish life, signaled a change in the attitude toward women in the Jewish society that came into direct contact with the Muslim world of that time. That Muslim world, on the basis of its religious teachings, forced women into a completely subservient role in family and social life. Education was denied to them, physical and verbal abuse was an accepted prerogative of the husband, polygamy was legitimized if not even encouraged, and a woman could be summarily divorced and sent away from the home without reason, recourse or appeal. It was in the seventh century that Jews arrived with the Muslim conquerors on the Iberian peninsula. These Jews from North Africa and Babylonia and the land of Israel became what is known as Sephardim. These Jews were very successful in Torah study, as well as commerce, politics, diplomacy and influence and for a number of centuries Spanish Jewry enjoyed a "golden era." Living in an originally total Muslim environment – albeit a fairly tolerant, progressive and educated one – the Jews naturally adopted many of the ways and attitudes of the Muslims toward women. We do not hear of any Jewish women scholars in that world and polygamy was tolerated but certainly not the norm in that Jewish society. The tradition of Jews generally was always one of monogamy and the Talmud, though never actually banning the institution of polygamy, did point out in its piquant fashion the inherent dangers and contradictions and problems to family life in such an arrangement of a polygamous home. Poetry was in fashion in the Spanish Muslim world of the time and therefore it appeared in the world of Spanish Jewry as well. A great deal of Jewish poetry was devoted to liturgy and religious subjects. However, as part of the poetic scene, poems regarding marriage, courtship and women were always part of the genre and such poems, some written by great and accepted Jewish poets and scholars, also were the norm. But though poems may have treated women idyllically, the vast majority of women remained basically uneducated and completely subservient in Spain's general and Jewish societies of the time.

Beginning in the late ninth century other Jews traveled from Babylonia and the Middle East up the Balkans eventually settling in the German Rhineland and France. These Jews came to be known as Ashkenazim, *Ashkenaz* being a biblical Hebrew name associated with Germany. These Jews lived in an oppressive, early Medieval, Roman Catholic environment. These Jewish communities were of small population and were constantly endangered by their Christian masters and neighbors and persecuted by the Church. Having none of the opportunities, culture or the freedoms of their Spanish brethren, the Ashkenazim engaged in a very limited commerce as money-lenders, vintners, merchants and laborers. No philosophers, doctors, court politicians, grammarians or poets for these *Ashkenazim*. Their entire intellectual thrust was in Torah and Talmudic studies. While the general non-Jewish medieval society idealized the upper-class woman, jousting for her favor or praising her in poetry and ennobling the concept of unrequited love, negative Christian attitudes toward women and marriage, including the creation of celibate orders and nunneries for women (to which some women were banished as punishment for unacceptable behavior), somehow combined with the loose morals of the peasant masses and created a contradiction in Christian society and its attitude toward relations between the sexes. This pattern of extreme prudishness on one hand, and then somehow followed or even accompanied by the other extreme of widespread licentiousness, haunted Christianity through all of the centuries; the West's current obsession with sexual matters is only a result of this millennia-long struggle within the soul of European and Western society as to these matters. The Christian medieval world was illiterate, violent, intolerant and superstitious. Thus the rational and holy society created by the early Ashkenazic Jews is even more remarkable than perhaps first observed or understood.

The major foundation for the Ashkenazic attitude toward women in their society was embedded in the decrees of Rabbeinu Gershom,

Me'or HaGola (The Light of the Exile). In the late tenth century he promulgated a number of decrees that shaped Ashkenazic Jewish life for a millennium. Prominent amongst these decrees was the practical abolition of polygamous marriages, the requirement of the woman's consent in a divorce procedure and the preference of *ḥalitza* (the alternate method of freeing a sister-in-law who has no children from the requirement of *yibum* – levirate marriage – to her brother-in-law after the death of her husband.) The decrees of Rabbeinu Gershom were not accepted by Sephardic Jewry until our time when, with the rise of the State of Israel, they became the law of that country. Rabbeinu Gershom's successors over the next two centuries created further decrees to protect women's monetary rights and to prevent their assets and families from being victimized by predatory husbands. Since the European Jewish communities of the time were small, close-knit and governed by religious figures and the rabbinical courts they headed, these decrees became relatively easy to enforce and appeals to outside communities and/or rabbis were almost always doomed to fall on deaf ears. The attitude toward women's education was also different than that of the Christian and Muslim worlds. Rashi's (Rabbi Shlomo Yitzḥaki, the premier Jewish commentator to the Bible and the Talmud) two daughters were well-known scholars and received great respect from their family and Rashi's disciples. Again, as with the women of the Talmud, it cannot be ascertained whether such women's education was widespread or whether Rashi's daughters were the exception. The widespread opinion among scholars is that Jewish education for women in the medieval world of France and Germany was fairly rare and that most Jewish women were as illiterate as their Christian counterparts. However, there is no real proof for this and in any event, the requirements of Jewish halakha required that women possess a basic knowledge of many Jewish laws, prayers and customs. It is obvious though that there were no formal schools for women in the Jewish society of the time. Nevertheless we find throughout Jewish history many instances of daughters of great scholars receiving a full Torah education from their fathers, especially when the family had no sons. From all of this we can gather that the attitude toward women's education in Jewish society was heavily influenced by the general non-Jewish societal attitudes of that particular time and place, and that this wavering, and seemingly contradictory attitude remained in constant and precarious balance within the Jewish world.

In Renaissance times, women played a greater role in Jewish Italy than in the other places of Jewish settlement. There are rabbinic responsa regarding Purim plays and costumes, balls and poetry that suggest that the greater freedom between the sexes that the Renaissance occasioned in Italy affected Jewish society as well. After the expulsion of the Jews from Spain in 1492, Sephardic Jewry largely became absorbed in the Muslim world. The role of Jewish women, though protected by halakhic norms and laws, was mainly one of little formal education and subservience to the men in their society. There were however exceptional women who wielded great influence. Foremost among these women was Dona Gracia Beatrice Mendes Nasi (Beatrice de Luna), a woman banker who defended her people and organized a boycott of the Papist port of Ancona in retaliation for the anti-Semitic acts of the Pope and the Church. Her boycott eventually failed mainly because Jewish merchants themselves refused to heed its call. She was also instrumental in having Rabbi Yosef Caro's *Shulḥan Arukh* (the basic book of Jewish law and custom composed in the sixteenth century) published and widely disseminated. She and her nephew Don Joseph Nasi (Duke of Naxos) acquired control over the city of Tiberias in the land of Israel and were active in attempting to establish a stronger Jewish presence in the country. Such remarkable women also appeared in the Ashkenazic communities in Europe, such as Glückel of Hamlin, a very well-educated and noted figure of her time who wrote extensive diaries about her Jewish life in Germany in the seventeenth century, but such women certainly were not the norm for the time and society. The wives of many noted rabbis were widely noted for their wisdom, advice and knowledge. Many legends about them and their sayings and activities abounded. They undoubtedly had influence over their husbands and thus indirectly over the community as well, but rarely were they active publicly in community or educational matters. The Jews in eastern Europe in the late Middle Ages and the early Modern Era lived in a surrounding society that was backward, poverty-stricken, repressive and brutal. Though the Jewish woman was not, as a rule, subjected to the physical abuses regularly visited on non-Jewish women, she remained basically uneducated and even sometimes illiterate and subject to the backbreaking and unending domestic household chores of that time and place. Life span was short, infant mortality high, and economic and educational opportunity was very limited and, in many instances, completely nonexistent. Yet it was somehow understood that the preservation of Judaism and the Jewish home lay directly within the province of the Jewish woman and her home.

With the advent of the ideas of the Enlightenment in the eighteenth century, things began to slowly change for women generally, especially in western Europe and eventually even in eastern Europe as well. The religious wars that wracked Europe in the previous centuries brought a general spirit of agnosticism and secularism to the intelligentsia of the time – a type of attitude of "plague on all of your religious houses." The Catholic Church declined in power and influence and by the time of the French Revolution at the end of the eighteenth century, women were in the forefront of the drive for greater personal freedom and democratic rule. Though Madame Defarge is a caricature of the time, there is no doubt that women's rights became more assertive in western European society as well as in the emerging countries of North America. The idea of universal suffrage had not yet gained hold but women owned property, took part in political debate, became better educated, attended special women's schools and began the long, slow climb up the ladder toward greater equality with their male counterparts. The wives of the early presidents of the United States such as Martha Washington and Dolly Madison were influential and powerful people. There were powerful queens of England such as Mary, Elizabeth I and Victoria. Though it was still a man's world (and my wife maintains that it still is) in almost all respects, the position of women in society, especially the higher echelons of it, was much improved over what it was in medieval times.

This change seeped into eastern European life as well. The rise of Hasidism in the eighteenth century, a revolution within the boundaries of halakha and tradition but a revolution nonetheless, facilitated a change in women's roles in Jewish society as well. In its earliest, most radical form, women were allowed a role in public Hasidic life. The daughter of Rabbi Yisrael Ba'al Shem Tov was herself regarded as a rebbe and conducted a Hasidic court of sorts. But by the 1840s the Hasidic world became the bastion of conservatism and women pretty much resumed the role that they had played previously. They remained basically uneducated and separate from public Jewish life. In Lithuania and White Russia where the advent of Hasidism was halted by the opposition of the Gaon of Vilna and other formidable rabbinic scholars, the ideas of the Enlightenment permeated. As a result, the status of women in these Jewish communities also began to change. In the nineteenth century, the women of the Jewish communities of Lithuania became better educated especially in the *Haskala* circles of the time but also in the deeply observant religious community as well. There were as yet no schools of formal Jewish education present, but the future could already be glimpsed. Also certain social changes occurred in Lithuanian Jewish religious society. On Simḥat Torah women descended to the men's section to observe the festivities and kiss the *sifrei Torah*. Rabbi Yechiel Michel Epstein in his monumental nineteenth-century work, *Arukh HaShulḥan,* admits that the tradition of married women covering their hair in public was no longer widely observed even in religious circles. Photographs of the time show that family seating at religious weddings and banquets was the norm. The ideas of the Enlightenment penetrated the Hasidic world as well. The winds of secularism, nationalism, Marxism and revolution blew strongly throughout eastern and central European Jewish life. Women were in the forefront of these movements and they flocked to attend the schools that were now open to them for their general education. The battle for the Jewish soul and future was being launched within the Jewish home itself as women now refused to remain uneducated and subservient.

After the disasters of the First World War that decimated European Jewry and destroyed much of its religious infrastructure, religious schools for women were founded. Telshe Yeshiva in Lithuania had a women's seminary, Yavneh, which was very popular and successful. Sarah Schenirer founded the Beis Yaakov school movement in Krakow, Poland in the early 1920s; a movement that eventually encompassed well over one hundred schools and thousands of students. Beis Yaakov was originally opposed by a number of rabbinic and Hasidic leaders but it gained the support of Rabbi Yisrael Me'ir Kagan and the Grand Rebbe of Gur. The rebbe stated that: "On the Sabbath eve, the father and the brother of the family attend my court and table-gathering while the daughter and sister attend the theater. How can the Jewish home survive in this fashion?"

Jewish women's education was the major revolutionary change in religious Jewish life of the twentieth century. Women teachers and even scholars became the norm in Jewish society. In the late 1800s, Rabbi Azriel Hildesheimer in Berlin was already conducting public classes and lectures in Torah subjects for women. Rabbi Yeḥiel Yaakov Weinberg gave limited sanction to Orthodox youth groups in the 1920s and 1930s in Germany where boys and girls both attended the same group. He saw it as a means of preserving this German Jewish youth for tradition and Orthodoxy. No such arrangement was ever sanctioned amongst the Hasidic communities of eastern Europe. Though the education of women was thus strongly encouraged, the social opportunities for women varied widely from community to community and from country to country. Women were far more active socially, and even politically, in western and Central European religious Jewish societies than in eastern Europe. But there is no doubt that the widespread availability of women's education gave religious women a different and more powerful sense of self than in previous centuries.

In the nineteenth and twentieth centuries the Reform and later Conservative movements distinguished themselves from Orthodoxy and tradition by allowing mixed seating in their temples and synagogues. This soon led to much more tinkering with halakha and traditional Jewish norms. In the second half of the twentieth century, overwhelmed by the fervor of feminism, these movements attempted to make radical changes in the status of women with regard to prayer services, intermarriage, matrilineal descent and social behavior. However, both movements are currently suffering from the assimilationist hemorrhage that is visiting them, and the attempt to save themselves with the championing of women is failing. Part of the social reality of life is that men view women differently to how women view themselves. A female former rabbi in a Conservative synagogue told me that she left her position when she realized that the congregation was more interested in the way she dressed than what she had to say. The rabbis of the Talmud who recognized the true psychological nature of men and women and society generally, and were the ultimate realists regarding human behavior, established a norm that to a certain extent dominates even over the legalities of pure halakha. That norm is called "*kavod hatzibbur*" – the honor of the congregation. By this they intended to preserve the decorum and the holiness of the prayer services and the public reading of the Torah. *Kavod hatzibbur* was meant to minimize and even prevent distractions during services. I have been told that this type of distraction is the fault of men and not of women. I will plead guilty to that charge. But nonetheless, the distraction is omnipresent and it is unrealistic to wish it away. The struggle to retrain the physical separation between men and women in prayer in the 1950s revitalized the Orthodox community in North America and has led to the continued growth of Orthodoxy against all predictions to the contrary.

In the twentieth century, women's educational opportunities further expanded. Women's colleges, seminaries, institutes, programs, classes, lectures, books and media products all became accepted in varying degrees throughout the Jewish world. Divisions in the Jewish religious world regarding such issues as family seating, studying of Talmud, women decisors and advisors, women holding public and communal office and other matters are still very present. There has been a strong movement, interestingly enough parallel to the growth of women's education and their ever-increasing entry into the professional and commercial world, to strengthen the social separation between the sexes in religious Jewish life. This is part of the swing of patterns in Jewish historical life and indeed, the great story of the Jewish people. Within halakhic boundaries, there are differing opinions and social customs regarding these issues. This is partly due to societal differences and varying customs inherited from past norms in eastern and western European communities. It can also be attributed to the radical change in the general Western society regarding the present extreme immodesty in dress, speech and behavior between the sexes that permeates our world. The rabbis taught us that one who sees a dissolute woman in her disgrace is entitled to take upon oneself the vows of being a *nazir* – a radical step of abstinence. In a general society of diminished moral norms or limitations, and a media that thrives on violence and immorality, it is understandable and even necessary to take preventive and defensive measures. Much of what we see in today's Jewish world regarding the limiting of social interaction of men and women is a direct response to the dissolute behavior and lack of moral norms in the general society.

There are still many unresolved issues regarding the status of women in Jewish society. Many of them are very complicated and not given to the simplistic solutions proposed by activists and publicists. But there is no doubt that the status of women in Jewish society today is far different than it was in past centuries. It is important to note that all of these changes in the status of women have been within the parameters of Jewish halakha. Many of the women's issues that are still in dispute and discussion today have differing opinions and support on all sides from recognized scholars and rabbis in the Orthodox Jewish world. As I indicated at the beginning of this chapter, these matters regarding women are very sensitive, delicate and critical. There is a definite pattern in the long Jewish story, an ebb and flow in the status and treatment of women in society. I am sure that the final chapter regarding these concerns has yet to be written and certainly not by me. But people living in the present should constantly be aware that there was a past and that there will be a future. The only certainty about life is a continued and omnipresent uncertainty, perpetual social change and the eternity of Torah and the people of Israel.

Chapter Six

The Land of Israel

Out of all of the patterns that appear in Jewish history perhaps the one that shows the least marked ebb and flow is the relationship of the Jewish people toward the land of Israel. Ensconced permanently and prominently in the thrice-daily prayers of the Jewish faithful, the return of the Jewish people was always a given in Jewish life; though, in practical terms, how and when such a return could occur was never clearly spelled out. For most of the years of the long exile of Jews from their homeland the longing for the return of the Jewish people to live again in the land of Israel was just that – a longing. The fulfillment of that longing was postponed, for the most part, to the messianic era and therefore the return to the land of Israel was to be somehow combined with supernatural and miraculous events. Yet individually, Jews immigrated to the land of Israel throughout the ages of the exile and there was a constant Jewish presence – unbroken though tenuous – in the land of Israel throughout the millennia of exile and dispersion. Maimonides maintained that such a presence was halakhically necessary in order for the workings of the Jewish calendar to operate in the absence of a Sanhedrin that would declare the new moon on a regular monthly basis. The situation of the Jews living in the land of Israel was always a precarious one. The Roman occupiers of the country were generally antagonistic toward Jews and Judaism, though there were short breaks during the reigns of Antoninus Pius and Marcus Aurelius when the Roman rule in Israel was more benign. But by the end of the fourth century when Christianity became the official religion of the Roman Empire, the enmity toward Jews, especially Jews living in the land of Israel, increased and deepened. The Byzantine Church, which dominated the eastern portion of the empire, embarked on a genocidal campaign against the Jewish population in the land of Israel, and the number of Jews living there declined precipitously with most fleeing to Egypt, North Africa and Babylonia. Eventually many Jews also reached the Iberian Peninsula, the Balkans and Provence, but a hard core hung on in the land and their personal tenacity assured a continuing Jewish presence in the land of Israel.

The Byzantine Christians were driven out of the land of Israel by the forces of Islam which rose in the seventh century. After the initial brutal attempts to coerce the Jews into accepting this new, Mohammedan faith failed, the Jews were afforded *dhimmi* status and adjusted to living as second-class residents in a Muslim society. The land of Israel was then sparsely settled and the Muslims built mosques on the Temple Mount to validate their claim to be the true religion of God. Jewish society and its scholars deferred to their large Jewish communal neighbor in Babylonia in all matters of Jewish law, scholarship and culture. Though the Jewish community in the land of Israel also contributed greatly in these matters, its contribution was dwarfed by the accomplishments of the Babylonian community and its yeshivot and scholars – the Geonim. The Jews of Babylonia were well established in the country, having lived there for over a millennium and evidently felt no compelling need to immigrate to the land of Israel, which was then under the rule of the caliphate in Baghdad. Instead, when the Babylonian Jews did leave Babylonia because of economic and other reasons, they traveled to North Africa, Italy, Spain, the Rhineland and France, and the Balkans as well, eventually settling in those locations. Thus was established a continuing pattern in the Jewish exile of intense, religious emotional longing to return to the land of Israel that somehow never was translated, for various reasons, into actual Jewish immigration in significant numbers, even when that option was socially and diplomatically possible and present.

In 1096 the Roman Catholic Church, motivated by assorted religious, geopolitical and economic incentives, proclaimed the First Crusade. This Crusade under the leadership of Godfrey of Boulogne destroyed the Jewish communities of the Rhineland, fought the Byzantine Christians of the East and eventually reached the land of Israel and Jerusalem. There it defeated the weak Muslim forces, forced conversions on the local population, turned the mosques on the Temple Mount into churches and destroyed the Jewish population of Jerusalem. The Jews in the rest of the country were also ruthlessly persecuted, with Jewish scholars regularly held as hostages for exorbitant ransoms. Thus the Jewish community in the land of Israel, small, defenseless, beleaguered and threatened with extinction, essentially went underground in order to preserve itself. The Muslims gradually reinfiltrated the country and, by the thirteenth century, the Christian kingdom of the Crusaders was no longer viable. Saladin, the Muslim ruler of Egypt and conqueror of Richard the Lionhearted and the Crusaders, allowed Jews to return to live in Jerusalem and Jewish life began to slowly revive. But the psychological trauma of the Crusades and its aftermath would haunt the Jews of the land of Israel and the world over for centuries to come. The failure of the Crusades to wrest the Holy Land from Muslim control must be seen as one of God's gifts to the Jewish history. It is highly unlikely that any Jewish state would have been able to arise in the land of Israel if it would have been under Christian dominance for many hundreds of years. Thirty years of harrowing British rule in the twentieth century pretty much proves this point. The official line of the world's main Christian groups was to oppose the creation of the State of Israel on theological grounds. It was only the weakness of the Muslim world at that time, coupled with British miscalculations that gave the Jews the opportunity to create their own state in 1948. David Ben Gurion was probably correct in his assessment that if the Jewish state were not declared and formed then another opportunity to do so in the normal course of world events would not possibly have arisen for many decades if not even centuries. In the anti-Jewish and anti-Israeli climate of the early twenty-first century, it is even clearer that his judgment was prescient.

Rabbi Yehuda HaLevi, the poet laureate of the Jewish people, left Spain in 1141 to immigrate to the land of Israel. His fate is unknown to us, though in Jewish legend he is enshrined as one of the great martyrs on behalf of the land of Israel, killed by an Arab horseman while bowing to the holy city of Jerusalem and its Temple Mount. He was representative of a continuing trickle of Jewish rabbinic leaders who made their way to the land of Israel in the Middle Ages. Rabbi Yeḥiel of Paris, one of the foremost Tosafists and scholars of the early thirteenth century, together with three hundred disciples and colleagues arrived in Israel and settled (under Crusader protection!) in Acre. But any mass Jewish immigration was precluded by economic, religious and logistical difficulties, such as the country's desolation and impoverishment, fierce and violent religious hostility from both Muslims and Christians against the Jews, and the long, difficult and dangerous nature of travel. In the late 1100s, Maimonides arrived in the land of Israel but, under the threat of kidnapping by Christian knights, he fled to the relative safety of Egypt. In 1267 the great Rabbi Moshe ben Naḥman (Ramban) left Spain and eventually settled in Jerusalem, founding there a synagogue still bearing his name today, though the original structure was destroyed long ago. His description of the desolation of the land and of the poverty and paucity of the Jewish population there is emotional and heartbreaking. Nevertheless, this barely noticeable trickle of Jewish immigration helped sustain Jewish life there during the Middle Ages, continuing the unbroken chain of Jewish life in the land of Israel from the time of Joshua.

In the early sixteenth century, in the aftermath of the tragic expulsion of the Jews from Spain, a relatively large immigration of Spanish Jews arrived in the land of Israel. They settled in Safed, Tiberias, Hebron and Jerusalem. Among the great men who led the Jewish people then were some of the most renowned scholars of Israel at that time – Rabbi Yaakov Beirav, Rabbi Yosef Caro, Rabbi Moshe Alshikh, Rabbi Isaac Luria (Ari), Rabbi Shlomo HaLevi Alkabetz, Rabbi Levi ibn Ḥaviv and Rabbi Yitzḥak Abuhav among others. There had not been such a large concentration of Jewish scholars in the land of Israel for almost a millennium. The influence of the famous Jewish woman financier Dona Gracia Beatrice Mendes Nasi and her nephew Don Joseph Nasi was very strong with the Turkish rulers of the country. In fact, the city of Tiberias and its environs were granted to Don Joseph as an independent Jewish fiefdom in the land of Israel. This development encouraged further Jewish immigration to the country, especially among Sephardic and converted Jews seeking to escape the yoke of Christendom. This period of the sixteenth century also marked the development and spread of kabbalistic thought – especially Lurianic kabbalistic ideas – from the land of Israel throughout the Jewish world. The fact that this type of Kabbala emanated from the Holy Land gave it added weight and authority in Jewish society and contributed greatly to its spread throughout the masses of the Jewish people. In spite of all of this early promise, by the end of the sixteenth century the Jewish community in the land of Israel had dwindled in terms of numbers and influence. There were many reasons for this, though internal rabbinic strife and deteriorating economic opportunities certainly contributed to this ebb of the Jewish tide there. Natural disasters such as plagues of disease reaching epidemic proportions, drought and earthquakes also wracked the country and continuing immigration reached a relative standstill. The bitter conclusion of the Shabbetai Tzvi chapter in Jewish history, when, in 1658, the proclaimed Jewish messiah converted publicly to Islam, also had a terribly negative effect upon world Jewry and any attempts to immigrate to the land of Israel in its immediate aftermath were put on hold. But still in the Jewish mind and heart, "Next year in Jerusalem" was a reality that never wavered.

At the dawn of the eighteenth century three hundred Polish Jews arrived in Jerusalem under the leadership and inspiration of Rabbi Yehuda HaḤasid. Rabbi Yehuda died almost immediately upon arriving in Jerusalem, but a small synagogue called Ḥurvat (the ruins of) Rabbi Yehuda HaḤasid was established, which has remained a famous Jewish landmark in the Old City of Jerusalem for generations. Rabbi Gershon Kitover, the brother-in-law of the founder of the Hasidic movement, the Ba'al Shem Tov, arrived in Jerusalem and Hebron in the eighteenth century with a group of his followers. There were Sephardic Jews who came to the land of Israel from the neighboring lands, all of which were under the control of the Ottoman Turks as was the land of Israel itself. Jews from the Caucuses and Bukhara, Yemen and Morocco, also found their way to the land of Israel and established their communities in Jerusalem and other areas of the country. Eventually, the Turkish rulers recognized this Sephardic community as the "official" community of the Jews and its rabbinic leader, called the Ḥakham Bashi, had restricted powers granted by the Turkish authorities. In the eighteenth century the Sephardim greatly outnumbered the number of Ashkenazic Jews living in the land of Israel. With the arrival of more Ashkenazim to the land, and especially to Jerusalem, in the eighteenth and nineteenth centuries, tensions arose between the Sephardic and Ashkenazic societies over various issues – many petty but some important. These tensions have not completely evaporated centuries later. The eighteenth century was a time of restlessness within the Jewish world. Under the pressure of modernism and Enlightenment the old norms of Jewish life and stability were weakened. The inexorable process of urbanization began to change Jewish life as well. The Hasidic revolution, the coming of *Haskala* and Reform, the growing poverty and persecution that were the lot of eastern European Jewry, all combined to create a feeling that the old conditions of Jewish life in the Diaspora were now changing. In this clouded and uncertain atmosphere Jews turned their eyes in a practical sense toward Zion and Jerusalem.

In the latter part of the eighteenth century, Rabbi Elijah Kramer, the famed Gaon of Vilna, attempted to leave Lithuania and immigrate to the land of Israel. Fate intervened and in Odessa he was unable to obtain transportation and thus returned to Vilna. However, many of his disciples and those he influenced did arrive in Jerusalem and Safed in the very early nineteenth century. They formed the backbone of the Ashkenazic community in Jerusalem and the country generally, and were the founders of what later would come to be called the "*yishuv hayashan*" – the old pre-Zionist Jewish community in Israel. Thus there began a small but steady immigration of Jews throughout the nineteenth century. Followers of Rabbi Shneur Zalman of Liadi, the founder of Chabad Hasidism, arrived as well as followers of Rabbi Moshe Sofer (Ḥatam Sofer) from Bohemia, Slovakia and Hungary who also took up residence in the Holy City. The Ashkenazim of nineteenth-century Jerusalem joined together to create a unified Beit Din court and rabbinate centered in the Old City of Jerusalem, though there always was continual strife among the different factions and groupings of Jerusalem's Ashkenazic community. Rabbi Shmuel Salant served as the rabbi of Jerusalem from 1839 till 1909 – a notable seventy years! He had many famous European rabbis who moved to Jerusalem during that period assist him in the physical and spiritual development of the community. By 1850 the Jews formed the majority population in Jerusalem. A wealthy and well-known Austrian Jew, Nisan Beck, undertook the construction of a large synagogue adjacent to where the Ḥurva of Rabbi Yehuda HaḤasid existed. This synagogue became the largest edifice in the Old City of Jerusalem excluding those on the Temple Mount. The Austrian Emperor Franz Joseph, when visiting Jerusalem later in the nineteenth century, contributed a generous donation toward the completion of the magnificent domed roof of that synagogue. This majestic structure was destroyed by the Jordanians and the Arabs in the War of Independence in 1948. The Ḥurva Synagogue, also destroyed in 1948 by the Arabs, was restored fully in 2010, while plans for restoring Nisan Beck's synagogue are currently in the making.

The land of Israel in the nineteenth century was a near wasteland with little economic opportunity available. It had a small population, arid soil and few natural resources. Tourism was practically non-existent and periodic plagues of trachoma, typhus, cholera and other diseases wracked the country. The Jews who immigrated to the country were supported by donations from Jewish communities in the Diaspora. This was in line with traditional Jewish belief and practice that Jews who lived in the land of Israel were entitled to such support by dint of their sacrifice in maintaining a Jewish foothold in the land. The Sephardic communities who spoke Arabic and were accustomed to Middle Eastern Muslim life were closer to a level of economic self-sufficiency than their Ashkenazic brethren who were thrust into a completely alien society. The Ashkenazim however had organized a fund-raising apparatus to funnel money to them from their eastern and central European places of origin. The charity was called the "Kupat Rabbi Me'ir Ba'al HaNes," and its yellow charity boxes were found in hundreds of thousands of Jewish homes throughout Europe and later America as well. The monies collected through this charity were smuggled into the land of Israel and a "*ḥaluka*" (division) system of the monies was devised to distribute the monies amongst the Ashkenazic population. There never was enough money to go around and the *ḥaluka* system invited nepotism, favoritism and corruption to infiltrate its institution. Nevertheless, the system did somehow work, after a fashion, throughout the nineteenth and part of the twentieth century and was the economic mainstay of many of the pious Jews of the *yishuv hayashan*. However, the *ḥaluka* system institutionally created and fostered a welfare-based and dependent mindset amongst many of its recipients, a mindset that still has not dissipated centuries after the system itself collapsed and ended.

In the latter decades of the nineteenth century there arose in eastern Europe, especially in Lithuania and Belarus, an organization called Hovevei Zion – The Lovers of Zion. This organization, which had many leading rabbis and scholars in its leadership such as Rabbi Naftali Tzvi Yehuda Berlin of Volozhin and Rabbi Shmuel Mohilever of Bialystok, encouraged larger Jewish immigration to the land of Israel and raised funds to support those Jews already living there. There were many *maskilim* – "enlightened ones" – and avowed secularists who were also part of the movement. It seemed that there was then a unity of thought and purpose regarding the land of Israel and its importance for Jewish life in eastern European Jewry that bridged ideological and religious observance differences. Among the secular notables of the Lovers of Zion was Dr. Leon Pinsker who had authored the treatise, *Auto-Emancipation*, which had a profound effect upon Jewish thinking and was a forerunner of the ideas of Herzl and political Zionism. Another work by a German Jew, Moses Hess, called *Rome and Jerusalem*, written in the mid-nineteenth century was also of influence in the Jewish world of the time and encouraged Jews to think of their future in terms of a national state of their own. The Hovevei Zion organization was boosted in its efforts by the enlistment of the French Baron Edmond de Rothschild to its cause through the efforts of Rabbi Shmuel Mohilever. From the 1870s until his death in 1937, Rothschild was the major private benefactor of Jewish settlements (then called colonies) and institutions in the land of Israel. He was therefore known as the "*Nediv HaYadua*" – the famous philanthropist. He founded the famed Carmel Wine Company in 1882 and eventually the vintners and workers in the winery formed a cooperative and the Baron gave them control of the company. The first bottle of wine produced by Carmel was sent as a gift to Rabbi Naftali Tzvi Yehuda Berlin as a token of recognition of his leadership role in Hovevei Zion. Rabbi Berlin, upon receiving the bottle of wine produced in the land of Israel by Jews observant of all of the agricultural laws pertaining to produce growing in the land of Israel, was so moved by the event that he changed into his Shabbat clothing to greet it! However, a dispute as to the correct halakhic method of dealing with the *shemitta* – the Sabbatical year of rest from agricultural work – greatly weakened the Hovevei Zion.

The question of the observance of the *shemitta* – the Sabbatical year every seven years – by the farmers working the land in the colonies of Baron Rothschild had arisen in the 1880s. For centuries on end there had never been major Jewish agricultural projects and intensive Jewish farming in the land of Israel. All of this changed with the new Jewish immigration and the colonies of Baron Rothschild. The Jewish farmers, almost all of them observant, demanded that Baron Rothschild support them financially during the *shemitta* year when they would not work the land. Baron Rothschild felt this to be an unreasonable demand and threatened to withdraw completely from the colonies project in the land of Israel. He requested that the great rabbis of the time somehow find a solution to this impasse. Under the instigation of Rabbi Shmuel Mohilever some of the leading halakhic decisors of the time, including Rabbi Yitzḥak Elḥanan Spektor of Kovno and Rabbi Dovid Karliner among other notables, devised a plan called *heter mekhira,* which allowed the Jewish-owned land in Israel to be sold to a Muslim, thus permitting certain types of Jewish labor on the land to be continued even in the *shemitta* Sabbatical year. The land would then be repurchased from the Muslim after the *shemitta* year had passed. The *heter mekhira* plan has been renewed in every *shemitta* year from the latter part of the nineteenth century through the beginning of the twenty-first century. The plan, however, engendered strong opposition from the rabbis of the *yishuv hayashan* in Jerusalem who preferred to rely on Arab-grown produce for the year. Rabbi Naftali Tzvi Yehuda Berlin also objected to the *heter mekhira* on the grounds that *shemitta* was then only a rabbinic ordinance, while selling Jewish land to a Muslim was, in his opinion, forbidden under Torah law. Rabbi Berlin then resigned from the Hovevei Zion organization and the leadership of the movement passed into secular Jewish hands led by Dr. Leon Pinsker. This signaled the beginning of the secularization of the movements to settle the land of Israel; the resultant more secular, nationalistic bent was the precursor of the secular Zionist movement founded by Theodor Herzl in 1897. In later times those who opposed the concept of *heter mekhira* constructed other halakhic methods to allow agricultural produce grown in the land of Israel to be farmed, grown, marketed and consumed in a *shemitta* year. The issue however, is still one of the major fault lines that divide sections of Orthodox Jewry one from another and from secular Jewry entirely.

In the early 1890s France and much of Europe was rocked and their attention riveted by the Dreyfus affair. As part of the continuing tension between Germany and France after the humiliating defeat of the French in the Franco-Prussian War of 1870, Germany successfully planted spies within the general staff of the French army. As the French began to close in on the suspected spies, these spies successfully fabricated documents and evidence pointing to the involvement of Captain Alfred Dreyfus, the sole Jewish officer attached to the general staff, as being the spy for Germany. Protesting his innocence, Dreyfus was nonetheless tried by a French court-martial and found guilty and sentenced to life imprisonment on Devil's Island. The trial was the sensation of European journalism of the time and Theodor Herzl, an assimilated Austrian Jew serving as the correspondent reporter on behalf of a famous Viennese newspaper, was assigned to cover the Dreyfus trial. Herzl was shocked and dismayed by the open and virulent hostility shown to Dreyfus particularly and to Jews generally by the French press, court and the mob on the street. Herzl was also distressed by the continuing anti-Semitic outbreaks and decrees of Czarist Russia. Herzl's strategic goal was to eliminate European anti-Semitism. His means of doing so was to "normalize" the Jewish situation. Herzl felt that anti-Semitism was caused by the fact that the Jews had no national trappings – no country of their own, no anthem, no legislature, no flag, etc. – but if these were present then the Jews would be "normal" like everyone else and anti-Semitism would soon disappear from the European scene. Building on the momentum for settling in the land of Israel provided by Jewish immigration and the efforts of the Hovevei Zion and Baron Rothschild, Herzl called for a general congress representing all Jewish factions to facilitate and plan the establishment of a Jewish national entity, a Jewish state. Under Herzl's leadership, the political Zionist movement was formed and the first Zionist Congress took place in 1897 in Basel, Switzerland. The Zionist movement was made up of disparate bedfellows ranging from the religious Mizrachi faction, to the secular and anti-religious Labor Zionists who were themselves split between Marxists, Socialists and anarchists. Nevertheless, Herzl managed to weld all of the different groupings into a powerful force and organization which strove for the return of the Jewish people in large numbers to their ancient homeland. Under Zionist auspices the Jewish National Fund was established and empowered to purchase land in then Palestine for Jewish settlement and development. The Zionist movement also sponsored the Keren HaYesod (lit. "foundation fund") to encourage Jewish development of the land of Israel and to finance immigration thereto. Thus was laid the basic organizational infrastructure for a Jewish state in the land of Israel.

Herzl attempted to enlist the help of the great powers of Europe to back the Zionist project. He was unsuccessful in these efforts and in fact, the Ottoman Empire which controlled the country at that time was especially hostile to his plans of attempting to create a Jewish state on Muslim territory. Nevertheless, in a weak moment, the corrupt Sultan of the Ottoman Empire offered to sell then Palestine to Herzl and the Zionists but nothing practical came of this illusion. There would be no easy way for a Jewish state to arise in the land of Israel. In 1904, England offered to help establish a Jewish state under its auspices in Uganda in central Africa. This offer split the Zionist movement in two, with Herzl and the mainly assimilated western European Jews willing to consider it while the eastern European Zionists led by Chaim Weizmann, all of them steeped in Jewish tradition though mostly no longer observant of Torah law, bitterly opposed it. For them it was the land of Israel only. Herzl staked his leadership and reputation on the adoption of this Uganda plan and as a personal vote of confidence in Herzl it was narrowly accepted by the 1904 Zionist Congress. Yet it also came to nothing in terms of practicality and action. Herzl, physically and emotionally drained, died soon thereafter at the age of forty-four. He had predicted in 1897 that a Jewish state would arise within fifty years. That seemingly outlandish prediction turned into a prophecy.

Jewish immigration to the land of Israel increased in the first decade of the twentieth century, though most eastern European Jews who immigrated went to North America. By the beginning of the First

World War in 1914 the Jewish population in then Palestine was more than eighty thousand. The First World War was to prove pivotal to the Jewish world generally and to the idea of Jewish settlement and statehood in the land of Israel particularly. By the end of the war, the Ottoman Empire, which had ruthlessly persecuted the Jews living in the land of Israel from 1914 to 1917, collapsed and the country was now under British occupation and rule. In 1917 the British Foreign Secretary Arthur Balfour had issued a letter expressing British support for the establishment of a Jewish national home in then Palestine. Chaim Weizmann, then residing in England, had been greatly influential in obtaining this declaration and sincerely believed that the road to Jewish statehood in the land of Israel passed through London and Whitehall. After the war ended, tens of thousands of Jews immigrated to the land of Israel and the building of the country began to take dynamic and rapid shape. By now the majority of Jews coming to the land of Israel were secular, leftist and determined to eradicate the influences of the Exile, whether positive or not, from their society and psyche. Though Mizrachi had strong rabbinic backing and enjoyed popularity in eastern European Jewish society, the majority of the rabbinic and Hasidic society of the time opposed the Zionist movement because of its secular anti-religious nature and did not encourage immigration to the land of Israel. Thus, the leadership of the Jewish *yishuv* passed into almost exclusively secular hands. This also reflects earlier patterns of Jewish history in the land of Israel where for long periods of time the Jewish community was led by idolaters, Sadducees and others who were not loyal to Torah and tradition. Nevertheless, in all of those incidents, traditional Judaism always rebounded and eventually gained ascendancy. This pattern is slowly emerging in present-day Israel as well.

In the time-honored fashion of governments appointing a Jew to carry out essentially anti-Jewish policies, Britain, which had obtained the mandate to govern Palestine from the League of Nations, appointed Herbert Samuel as the first High Commissioner for Palestine. Britain immediately began backing away from its Balfour Declaration commitments. In 1922 it split off Trans-Jordan and gave it to the Hashemite family as its kingdom. There were Arab anti-Jewish riots in 1920, 1923, 1926 and 1929, which led to British restrictions on further Jewish immigration into the country. In the 1920s the secular Zionists, in cooperation with the British authorities, controlled the issuing of immigration certificates to Palestine. Nevertheless there was substantial immigration of religious Jews to the country in spite of secular and some rabbinic opposition. The great yeshiva of Slobodka and its leaders and students arrived in 1923, and settled first in Jerusalem and then later in Hebron. Thousands of Hasidim of Gur also arrived then as did other groups mainly, though not exclusively, sponsored by the Mizrachi and HaPoel HaMizrachi movements. The *yishuv* expanded greatly in the 1920s and 1930s and truly created a pre-state infrastructure. It organized a defense force to help ward off the continuing Arab attacks against Jews and Jewish settlements. All of this was accomplished in the face of growing British hostility toward the *yishuv* and the Zionist idea generally, as Britain reversed course and, in the 1930s, greatly restricted Jewish immigration into the country. This coincided with the rise of Hitler and was thus the cruelest of policies for it condemned many thousands to death by shutting the doors of the land of Israel in their faces. The Peel Commission of 1936 already recommended a partition of the country between Arabs and Jews under British rule, and the British White Paper of 1939 restricted Jewish immigration into the country even further. By the start of World War II, the Jewish population in the land of Israel numbered half a million souls while the Arab population was three times that. Yet the Arabs were disorganized and given to bitter clashes and disputes among warring clans and tribes. The Arab leaders, such as Haj Amin al Husseini, the Grand Mufti of Jerusalem, openly sided with the Axis powers in their war against the Western Allies. Nonetheless, British policies and behavior toward the Jews of then Palestine remained hostile and restrictive. Britain played the numbers game and the oil game and, therefore, in its own perceived self-interest, backed the Arabs against the Jews and ignored its previous commitments and promises. The pattern of history is that one should never trust governments on their previous word. The *yishuv* learned this truth in a bitter and painful measure.

In response to the growing hostility of Britain toward Zionism and the *yishuv*, there arose paramilitary groups amongst the Jews who were determined to end the British rule in the country. Though the official Zionist movement distanced itself and at times actively opposed these groups, the militant Jewish organizations received wide support and sympathy. The largest group was the Irgun Tzva'i Le'umi (Etzel) eventually led by Menachem Begin, a Polish Jew who had been imprisoned in Russia and eventually made his way illegally into the land of Israel. A second smaller group was called Loḥamei Ḥerut Yisrael (Leḥi). The British contemptuously called it the Stern Gang after the name of its leader Avraham Stern. The heads of the Jewish *yishuv* also had an organized defense force called Hagana. As is also the pattern in Jewish history, these disparate groups spent time and effort disagreeing with each other and sometimes even actually fighting one another. It was not until the middle of the War of Independence that all of the groups were disbanded and a united Israel Defense Force was created. Under the pressure of guerilla warfare against its troops and the dire economic situation of the British Empire, Britain relinquished its control over Palestine and tossed the problem into the lap of the United Nations, which again decreed a partition of the small country between the Jews and Arabs. The Jews accepted the plan but the Arabs rejected it vowing to drive the Jews out of the country completely. From 1947 (even though the State of Israel was not declared until May 14, 1948) to 1949 the War of Independence raged, with the Jews emerging as the unlikely victor of that struggle. After almost two thousand years a Jewish sovereignty was reestablished in the land of Israel. There were about 600,000 Jews living in the newly founded state in 1948.

Jewish refugees from the remnants of European Jewry who had survived the Holocaust, and hundreds of thousands of Jews who were driven out of their ancestral homes by Muslim mobs and Arab governments, immigrated to the State of Israel. The Jewish population numbered over two million within a decade of the founding of the state. World Jewry rallied to the aid of the fledgling nation and, in spite of continuing Arab violence and terrorism, enormous problems of integrating the new immigrants, and the continuing enmity and hostility of the Soviet bloc to its existence, the State of Israel survived and began to flourish.

As the state grew and prospered, traditional patterns of dispute arose once more in the Jewish world regarding its meaning. Some saw the state as a purely secular nationalistic enterprise. Many saw it as a refuge place for dispossessed Jews the world over but without any particular national or religious importance. Some believed it to be the beginning of the prophetic promise of ultimate redemption and messianic hope. Still others objected to its very existence as a contravention of Jewish theology, an argument originally advanced against the Zionist movement in earlier times. Over time, being anti-Israel became fashionable in the diplomatic and political sphere of world politics. It also gained a firm foothold in the world's academic circles and eventually infiltrated the Jewish world as well with Jewish academics, leftists and extreme liberals turning against the very existence of the state itself. Nevertheless, by the beginning of the twenty-first century there were almost six million Jews living in the land of Israel and the state was a considerable military and economic power. The Arab-Israeli confrontation showed no signs of easing but the centrality of the land of Israel continued unabated. As the great Rabbi Levi Yitzḥak of Berditchev said regarding God Himself: "One can be for God. One can be against God. But no one can ever be without God!" Well, the same may be paraphrased regarding Israel and the land of Israel in our time: "One may support the State of Israel. One may object to the State of Israel. But no one can ignore the existence of the State of Israel." The eternal pattern of Jewish attachment throughout the ages to the land of Israel remains unaffected by the passage of time and the vagaries of circumstance.

One of the great misconceptions regarding the State of Israel, a concept unfortunately furthered by the inept Israeli public relations establishment itself, is that the State of Israel is a product of the Holocaust and that its legitimacy is based upon a UN resolution. As I hope this chapter has abundantly shown, the State of Israel is the product of an unbroken millennia-long relationship between the Jewish people and its homeland. The Holocaust bought temporary world sympathy for the Jewish return to the land of Israel, but the Holocaust is not the basis of Jewish legitimacy in the land of Israel. That legitimacy is based upon a continuous Jewish settlement in the country for over three millennia and a perpetual loyalty to the land during all of the long night of Jewish exile and wanderings. I am always amazed that the State of Israel takes important visitors to the country firstly to the Holocaust memorial museum as though that is why they should support us in our existential struggle in the land of Israel. Instead these visitors should be taken immediately to the Temple Mount, the City of David, the Cave of the Patriarchs and Matriarchs, etc.; we are not a people of the Holocaust alone. We are a nation of Mount Sinai and Jerusalem, of Joshua and David, of the pioneer settlers of Palestine in the eighteenth and nineteenth centuries and of a people who have returned to their never-abandoned homeland and made it fertile and prosperous once more. And Jewish belief and Torah law made it clear that only in the land of Israel would the people of Israel find eventual spiritual and national fulfillment. The Holocaust illustrated how necessary a Jewish state is for the survival of world Jewry. But the legitimacy of the State of Israel in the land of Israel is completely independent of the Holocaust. In his testimony before the British Peel Commission in 1936, David Ben Gurion stated that "our deed of ownership of the land of Israel is the Bible." Would that the Jewish people believed that and acted in accordance with that belief.

Chapter Seven

Messianism and Mysticism

The belief in a messiah who will usher in an age of peace and tranquility for Israel and mankind generally, is one of the core tenets of Judaism. Maimonides records it as one of the thirteen basic beliefs of Jewish faith. The concept of a messiah existed in Jewish life long before the Jewish people were driven from their land and the Temple was destroyed. The Talmud records for us that King Ḥizkiyahu of First Temple Judah was deemed to be worthy of being the messiah and therefore much of Jewish and world history could have been short-circuited. The messiah is inextricably linked to King David who was the king anointed by the prophet Samuel (the name messiah literally means "one who is anointed"), and the messiah is therefore necessarily deemed to be a direct descendant of this Davidic line and pedigree. The destruction of the First Temple was a tremendously traumatic blow to the Jewish people and its psyche. However, since the prophets of Israel had predicted that the Babylonian exile would be a relatively short one – seventy years – the return of the Jewish people to the land of Israel and to Jerusalem and the rebuilding of the Temple were not seen as messianic events. Ezra, Nehemiah, Mordekhai, and the Men of the Great Assembly were seen as great heroes but not as messianic personalities. The prophets and scholars of Israel at the beginning of Second Temple times were aware that the Second Temple was also doomed to eventual destruction 420 years later, and thus one of the key elements of messianic times – permanence and eternity – was not present. The Second Temple was deemed "greater" than the First Temple because it stood for a decade longer, but it always had a feeling of impending doom hovering over it. Ezra was comparable to Moses in the eyes of the Talmud but he was not the messiah, not only because he was not descended from King David (he was a Kohen descended from Aaron and the tribe of Levi while David was descended from the tribe of Judah), but because impermanence of the Temple and the Second Commonwealth was instinctively recognized within Israel.

The entire period of the Second Temple was one of unending turmoil in Jewish society. In 325 BCE Alexander the Great arrived in the land of Israel and, though he did not destroy the country or the Temple and did not exile its Jewish inhabitants, he did convert the society to one of Greek culture and political domination. By the year 170 BCE the Temple was defiled with statues of Greek gods erected within its premises. A large portion of the Jewish population, especially the upper class and a section of the priesthood itself, were completely Hellenized, and collaborated with the Syrian Greek authorities to attempt to eradicate Judaism and a Torah way of life from the land of Israel. In 165 BCE, the Maccabees mounted a successful revolt against the Syrian Greek rulers of the country as well as against the Hellenized Jews, and ruled the country for the next 104 years. But again none of the Maccabees was ever deemed to be a messiah (they were also Kohanim descended from Aaron and the tribe of Levi.) As long as the independent Jewish state existed there apparently there was little longing for the messiah in practical terms. However, in 64 BCE, Pompeii, the Roman general and later emperor, entered Jerusalem and placed the land of Israel under Roman domination with puppet "Jewish" rulers (they were descended from Idumean leaders who were forcibly converted to Judaism by the Maccabees; the rabbis designated them to be of questionable Jewish pedigree) doing the bidding of Rome. With this worsening of the political situation of the Jews in the land of Israel, messianic longings began to intensify.

The first century BCE was a time of deep divisions in the Jewish community in the land of Israel. The rabbis and traditionalists were represented in the group known as Pharisees. They preached an avoidance of conflict with Rome's temporal power, a strict adherence to Torah law and a devotion to the study of Torah above all else. It was this group that continued the development and popularization of the Oral Law that eventually resulted in the Mishna and the Talmud. The Hellenized Jews morphed into the group known as Sadducees. They denied the authority and even the authenticity of the Oral Law, were powerful and wealthy, cooperated with Roman authorities and were open to Roman ways, culture, sports and policies. The Pharisees naturally believed in the messiah's eventual coming but did not tie that coming to a release from the then current Roman yoke of oppression. According to their beliefs, the period of messianic redemption had not yet arrived and they felt that any overt opposition to Roman rule would prove to be foolhardy and eventually disastrous to the Jews. A third group in Jewish society then, small in number but of some influence nevertheless, was the Essenes. An ultra-pious, mainly celibate society, given to daily purifications in pools of water, they had apocalyptic visions of the imminent arrival of the "end of days" and thus necessarily of the advent of the messiah. It is from this group that John the Baptist and other early Christians arose.

There is a pattern that continues throughout Jewish history regarding these groupings. The mainstream traditional community has always had to fight off the groupings that were largely otherworldly and messianic in behavior, and attitude, as well as confronting other strong, sometimes even dominant groups that were mainly non-observant of Torah ritual in daily behavior, and who denied the divinity of that Torah law and of Talmudic interpretation of Judaism. Jewish life has been tortured by false messiahs that arose constantly in its midst over the ages. And from the Hellenists, Sadducees, Karaites, Renaissance lovers, *Haskala* (the enlightened ones), Reform, Conservative, secular groupings, Marxists and new-age Leftists, traditional Jewry and its view of Judaism has continually been under attack and ridicule. Though traditional Judaism has weathered all such attacks and survived strong and proud, its attackers have periodically disappeared from the scene only to reappear again, morphed into a differently named entity but still clinging to the basic denial of Torah divinity and the necessity for the observance of ritual law. All of these groupings exist today in current

Jewish life, each claiming authenticity and power. Though I have written about these groupings in an earlier chapter, I mention this subject now for it is closely related to mysticism and messianism in Jewish life.

At the beginning of the Common Era, messianic expectations were fanned in the Jewish world by Roman persecution, by the erection of the immensely beautiful and ornate Second Temple in Jerusalem by Herod, and by the strange appeal of ascetic Essenian life to many Jews. In such a combustible situation, a person claiming not only to be the messiah but even a son of God arose. Though actual historical facts about Jesus of Nazareth are sparse, he became the central figure in Christianity, a religion that sprung from Judaism but rapidly departed from its original Jewish roots. Jesus was portrayed as the super messiah who suffered for all humanity's sins, and in Trinitarian doctrine is part of God, so to speak. He did not come to rescue Israel from the clutches of Rome (he was not a particularly Jewish messiah), but rather to redeem all of mankind from sin and bring the heavenly kingdom down to earth. The Jews rejected him as the messiah since (a) he died early in his career and a dead messiah is unable to fulfill his mission; (b) God has no parts; (c) no messianic benefits accrued to mankind after his appearance; and (d) there is no room in Judaism for a replacement revelation that would supersede the revelation at Sinai to Moses and Israel. There is no more devastating accusation that can occur than maintaining that one's messiah is nothing of the sort, and the Jews have paid dearly at Christian hands for millennia for their denial of Jesus' messianic persona. This is the prime example in Jewish and world history of the effect of messianism unfulfilled in human events. It also marks the beginning of Jewish wariness regarding messianism and its inherent dangers. As more false messiahs proliferated over the centuries of Jewish life this wariness increased.

Jesus may have died but Jewish messianism did not end there. Barely a few generations after the early rise of Christianity and the destruction of the Second Temple by the Romans, another messianic fervor swept Jewish society. Messianism grows in the soil of national tragedy. All of the great tragedies of Jewish history have given rise to messianic hopes and movements. In the second century CE, Shimon ben Kosiba, popularly known as Bar Kokhba, mounted a rebellion against Roman rule in the land of Israel. The rebellion was initially successful, even recapturing Jerusalem and planning to rebuild the Temple. Shimon proclaimed himself as the messiah and received wide popular support and veneration as such. Even Rabbi Akiva, the greatest sage of the time, endorsed his messianic ambitions and supported him. Other rabbis of the time disagreed, saying to Rabbi Akiva: "Akiva, you will be in your grave and the messiah will still not have arrived!" Sadly this prediction proved accurate. Bar Kokhba was eventually killed and his supporters scattered and exiled, and many of them, including Rabbi Akiva, savagely executed by the Romans. The failed messianic drive resulted in the complete destruction of Jerusalem, in the leveling of the Temple mount, and the persecution of Jews and Judaism for the next generation of Roman rule. As the rest of this chapter will show, a failed and false messiah is far worse for Jewish interests than no messiah at all.

The rise of Islam in the seventh century CE and the continuing oppression of the Jews by both the Byzantine Eastern Orthodox and the Roman Catholic Churches gave rise to a number of false messiahs, mainly in Iraq and Yemen in the early Middle Ages. Maimonides decried their claims and warned the Jews not to be taken in by them – he called them charlatans and evil. These false messiahs did not really amount to much and had scant popular support. But the spirit of messianism still lurked always beneath the surface of Jewish life. People who claimed to be representatives of the lost Ten Tribes of Israel such as Eldad HaDani and David HaReuveni surfaced and gained credence in both the Jewish and non-Jewish world. Eldad appeared in the tenth century in Iraq, and David in the fifteenth century in Italy and Spain. Both claimed that they were emissaries from the lost Ten Tribes and were heavenly inspired messengers regarding the impending arrival of the messiah of Israel. Eldad is still remembered for a number of rulings of Jewish ritual law attributed to him. David died in the prison of a Christian nobleman after being hailed by the Jews and even being granted an audience with the Pope of Rome. The failure of the messiah to arrive discredited them and their message, but still the spirit of messianism amongst Jews was present. In practical effect it was codified into a principal belief and tenet of Judaism itself by Maimonides who included it in his famous and authoritative list of the thirteen cardinal beliefs of Judaism. In the age of Maimonides there were a number of false messiahs that appeared in the Jewish communities of the Middle East. Maimonides himself wrote polemics against these false messiahs. Yet he himself proposed a date, falling in the thirteenth century, when the messiah would arrive. This ambivalent attitude toward the messiah's arrival – the denunciation of claimed messiahs and yet the constant longing for the messianic redemption – is reflected in the wording of Maimonides regarding the coming of the messiah. Thus Maimonides warned that even though the arrival of the messiah may not be imminent – he may tarry – one should yet ever hope and believe daily that he will arrive. And this has been a basic Jewish belief undimmed by time and circumstance till today.

Jewish messianism has always been intertwined with Jewish mysticism. According to Jewish tradition, the fundamental worldview and ideas of Jewish mysticism are derived from the work and teachings of Rabbi Shimon bar Yoḥai, the disciple of Rabbi Akiva and one of the leading scholars of the Mishna, though the concepts involved are part of the tradition of revelation from Sinai. This is popularly known as Kabbala – literally meaning "a received tradition." Kabbala was a private study, known to some scholars and holy men and never revealed for public use or the study halls of the masses. This tradition of secrecy began to break down in the early Middle Ages, especially in Spain, Germany and Provence. In the eleventh, twelfth and thirteenth centuries the *ḥasidei Ashkenaz,* the holy and pious men of Germany, flourished under the leadership of Rabbi Yehuda HaḤasid and others. In Provence, Rabbi Yitzḥak "*Sagi Nahor,*" the son of the famed Ra'avad of Posquières was a well-known kabbalist in the thirteenth century as were other well-known scholars of that time and place. In Spain, Rabbeinu Baḥya and the famed Rabbi Moshe ben Naḥman (Ramban) wrote commentaries to Torah and included within them specific sections dedicated to kabbalistic concepts and worldview. Kabbalistic thought spread throughout the Jewish world. Kabbala supplied otherworldly answers to problems and persecutions in the Jewish world which rational and natural thought and logic could not. Due to the increasing and apparently never-ending problems of exile and persecution, it was natural for Jewish mysticism to flourish and grow. There is no reference to Kabbala in the works of Rashi or Maimonides or for that matter in the Talmud itself. There were other great scholars in Spain, France and Provence who decried the popularization and spread of Kabbala among the masses. Nevertheless, the acceptance of Kabbala as being holy and legitimate in Jewish society was nearly unanimous.

In the fifteenth century, a Spanish Jew by the name of Moshe de Leon published a kabbalistic work called *Zohar*. He claimed to have copied it from the original manuscript of Rabbi Shimon bar Yoḥai. Much controversy has raged over the ages about the authenticity of Moshe de Leon's claim. His own wife stated that her husband was himself the author of *Zohar* and that he merely ascribed it to Rabbi Shimon bar Yoḥai in order to gain credibility for the work. In the eighteenth century, Rabbi Yaakov Emden stated that the ideas formulated in the work were from Rabbi Shimon bar Yoḥai, though the work itself was that of Moshe de Leon. Be that as it may, the book gained wide distribution and popularity in the Jewish world and became and remains the basic book of kabbalistic thought and interpretation. The attempt by Maimonides to convert Judaism into a purely rational, logical and philosophically based faith failed in the face of the spread of Kabbala and *Zohar* throughout the Jewish world. There would remain pockets within traditional Jewry that would shy away from studying *Zohar* or accepting kabbalistic ideas and thought patterns, but they would remain a definite and almost silent minority. Thus mysticism joined its sister, messianism, as a potent force in Jewish society, life and worldview. Kabbala became the expression of Jewish philosophy in the late Middle Ages and early modern era. Probably the most potent example of this symbiosis is to be found in the works of the sixteenth-century rabbi of Prague, Rabbi Yehuda Loewe (Maharal) and his disciples. This soon became the norm in late medieval and early modern Jewish commentaries to Torah, combining the mystical and the unknown with the rational and revealed truths of Torah into one apparently seamless whole.

The tragedies of 1391 – a nationwide Spanish pogrom – and 1492 – the expulsion of the Jews from Spain – together with the persecution of the Converso Jews by the Inquisition, naturally raised messianic hopes amongst Jews. According to legendary tradition, great troubles must occur directly before his coming. Various forerunners of the messiah appeared, chief among them, Shlomo Molkho, a convert to Judaism who delved in mysticism and was considered a holy soul by many later scholars and who was executed by the Inquisition, was a well-known person of the times. However, it was in the aftermath of the expulsion of the Jews from the Iberian Peninsula that kabbalistic thought spread throughout the Jewish world. It seemed to be the only avenue of thought that provided any sort of answer to the great misfortune that had befallen the Jewish world and to give that misfortune a positive spin. This was especially true of the Spanish exiles who reached the land of Israel where many of them settled in Jerusalem and in Safed. Rabbi Yaakov Beirav, a noted Spanish scholar and the mentor of Rabbi Yosef Caro, author of the *Shulḥan Arukh*, felt that the generations after the Spanish expulsion would see the arrival of the messiah. As such, he attempted to reintroduce into Jewish life the establishment of the Sanhedrin – the highest court and halakhic authority in Judaism – as a necessary precursor to the advent of the messiah. As can be imagined, this proved to be very controversial, the Sanhedrin therefore never gained the necessary halakhic and rabbinic authority to be truly effective, and the idea itself died aborning.

The great explosion of Kabbala throughout the Jewish world took place in the late sixteenth century under the impetus of the great mystic and holy man Rabbi Isaac Luria, known by his acronym, ARI. His system of Lurianic Kabbala differed from the ideas of his predecessors and attempted to answer many of the questions that beset the minds of Jews the world over – the length and bitterness of the Exile, the purpose of suffering, the scattering of Jews over the entire world, the secrets of nature and creation, etc. – and his ideas proved to be wildly popular amongst the scholars and masses of Israel. The Ari made the mystical world the real world for many Jews and paved the way for the rise of the Hasidic movement in eastern Europe in the eighteenth century. Sephardic Jewry also adopted the study of *Zohar* and of Lurianic Kabbala as being basic to its life of faith and observance. Kabbala thus now became the property of the masses of the Jewish people, something which would have mixed blessings in the immediate future.

In 1648–9 an immense pogrom led by the Ukrainian nationalist Bogdan Chmielnicki engulfed eastern European Jewry. Hundreds of thousands of Jews were killed, maimed or driven and displaced from their homes, families and communities. A tragedy of this proportion naturally once again reignited messianic hopes and longings. And within the decade after the pogrom a false messiah did in fact arise. He was a Turkish Jew, Shabbetai Tzvi, a man of brilliance and charisma, and also suffering from a manic-depressive psychological disorder. From 1653 to 1658 he dominated the stage of the Jewish world and, to a certain extent, even of the non-Jewish society. He had a great publicist, Nathan of Gaza, who helped to spread Shabbetai's fame and develop an enormous following throughout the Jewish world. Those who opposed him were pilloried and persecuted. His main opponent, a feisty rabbi in Amsterdam by the name of Yaakov Sasportas, was driven from the city by the irate believers in Shabbetai Tzvi. Gershom Scholem, the modern-day scholar who wrote extensively on the events of that time, attributed Shabbetai's initial success to the spread of Lurianic Kabbala throughout Jewish society. Other scholars are more skeptical of that claim. Be that as it may, the entire messianic fervor collapsed when Shabbetai converted to Islam. The devastating effect that this act of perfidy had on the Jewish world cannot be overestimated. It is no exaggeration to state that the events of the Jewish world over the next three centuries were all somehow related and a reaction to this failed false messiah and the attendant discrediting of messianism as being an answer to Jewish national problems. Even after his apostasy, pockets of true believers in Shabbetai as the messiah remained in the Jewish world. Another false messiah, Yaakov Frank, arose in Poland at the beginning of the eighteenth century and he in turn converted to Catholicism with hundreds of his followers under the pressure of the Polish authorities of the time. These events certainly gave traditional messianism a bad name in the psyche of the Jewish world and also evoked a backlash against the widespread use of Kabbala by the masses of Israel.

Rabbi Yaakov Emden led the charge against those suspected of having Sabbatean tendencies. He also joined those who opposed the works of Rabbi Moshe Ḥayyim Luzatto, an Italian kabbalist who was banned by leading Italian and French rabbis because of his open and practical use and espousal of Kabbala and its methodology in daily life. However, because of his magisterial work, *Mesilat Yesharim*, (*The Path of the Righteous*), Rabbi Luzatto was rehabilitated by the Gaon of Vilna and later by the *Musar* movement, so that all of his works are now mainstays of the yeshivot and women's seminaries. History has the last vote on policies and people, raising some of them from previous criticism and lowering others from previous glory and approbation. Kabbalistic study retreated to the confines of the scholars once more and traditional ideas of messianism became taboo in the Jewish world.

But a new form of messianism would soon arise – a secular messianism if you will – based on the ideas of the European Enlightenment of the eighteenth century. The Enlightenment spawned beliefs in deism, agnosticism and atheism in the intellectual classes of European society. It mocked and derided traditional religious beliefs, structures and institutions. Belief in democracy, tolerance, equality and fraternity heralded this new messianism. No longer was the messiah to be a person but rather it was to be an idea and a political system that would transform human society and usher in the golden age of humanism, peace and mutual cooperation. The better world was within reach. This form of messianism reached the Jewish world as well in the eighteenth century, taking on the form of Reform in Germany and central Europe and of *Haskala*/Enlightenment in eastern Europe. Kabbala was completely rejected by the "enlightened ones," and only logic and rationality prevailed. Berlin became the new Jerusalem and the traditional idea of a messianic redemption of the Jews from the long exile was derided and ignored. Secular messianism would allow Jews to live as equal and proud citizens of any country in which they resided and promised a world free of anti-Semitism and discrimination. Again, history, which has the last word on all of these matters, proved that secular messianism was hollow, illusory and as false a messiah as was Shabbetai Tzvi.

The rise of the Hasidic movement in eastern Europe in the eighteenth century reinvigorated the ideas of mysticism and Kabbala amongst the Jewish population. The opponents of Hasidism such as the Gaon of Vilna were also well versed in Kabbala. However, they strenuously objected to its spread and popularization amongst the masses of Israel. They also objected to the changing of ritual and custom to conform to kabbalistic ideas. Nevertheless, Hasidism spread rapidly throughout eastern Europe and eventually represented the vast majority of eastern European Jewry. Hasidism was not monolithic but all of its branches subscribed to a kabbalistic worldview and practiced kabbalistic customs, studied *Zohar* regularly and, in fact, inserted paragraphs of the

Zohar itself into daily and Shabbat prayers. This had been the practice of Sephardic Jewry already for many generations. Many of these prayers were adopted by even the non-Hasidic groups of eastern European Orthodoxy with German Orthodoxy being the exception to this practice. Thus mysticism became a more dominant force in Jewish religious life. Pilgrimages to receive blessings from holy people and Hasidic masters, visits to the graves of the righteous, formulae to combat the effects of the "evil eye," and other such mystical practices all became de rigueur in everyday Jewish life and continue to be nowadays in many Jewish circles. The study and practice of Kabbala today remains immensely popular in the Jewish – and even in parts of the non-Jewish – world.

The idea of a secular messianic era took root once again with the establishment of secular Zionism by Theodor Herzl in 1897. Religious Zionism also began then, but its founder, Rabbi Yitzḥak Yaakov Reines, was careful not to attribute any messianic overtones to it in its inception. However, later religious Zionists and especially Rabbi Avraham Yitzḥak Kook, the founding Chief Rabbi of Palestine in the 1920s, saw in the rise of Zionism, in the Balfour Declaration, in the large Jewish immigration to the land of Israel, and in the British mandate over Palestine after the enormous cataclysm of the First World War, the forerunner of messianic times. With the coming of the independence of the State of Israel after the unbelievably horrific events of the Holocaust this messianic feeling spread and grew. It reached apocalyptic proportions after Israel's stunning victory in the 1967 Six Day War and the reunification of Jerusalem under Jewish sovereignty. The religious Zionist movement saw and sees in the State of Israel clear manifestations of the advent of the messianic era. It is what fueled the settler movement and the establishment of Jewish communities throughout Judah and Samaria. Needless to say, other non-Zionist Orthodox groupings do not agree to this prognosis and much of non-Orthodox and secular Jewry also distances itself from messianic beliefs generally and any messianic qualities of the State of Israel particularly.

Maimonides, following the opinion of Mar Shmuel in the Talmud, foretold a rather bland and natural messianic era. Israel would be freed of the domination and influence of foreign powers over it but otherwise life and nature would continue as always. Maimonides differentiates the messianic era from the time of the revival of the dead and from the World to Come. He posits definite tasks that the messiah will fulfill but states that he will die and be succeeded by his descendant. The great prophesies of Isaiah about the lion and the lamb living together are only allegories in his opinion and not to be taken literally. In short, he foresaw a messianic era brought about through ordinary and non-miraculous events. Due to the length and severity of the exile and the enormous cost in lives and material of the Jewish people, Jews generally were unwilling to accept the idea of such a colorless messianic era. Based on kabbalistic ideas and various traditions and legends, the messianic era therefore took on apocalyptic proportions in Jewish society. The time of the revival of the dead and the World to Come were all merged into the messianic era; the messiah would perform wondrous acts, punish the wicked and reward the righteous and banish all evil and illness from the world. He would redeem the Jews from all prejudice and discrimination and rebuild the Temple in Jerusalem and create an eternal Jewish state in the land of Israel. The prophesies of Isaiah and the other prophets of Israel regarding the messianic era would all be fulfilled literally, nature would change and the world would be restored to its state of being as it was before the sin of Adam and Eve in the Garden of Eden. These beliefs certainly raised the bar for any potential messiah. To a certain extent this standard of messianism lies behind the ambivalent attitude that many believing Jews have toward the secular State of Israel of today. It does not fit their picture of what the messianic era is supposed to look like.

The latter part of the twentieth century saw a resurgence of interest in Kabbala in both the Jewish and non-Jewish world. It became part of New Age thought and the search for life's meaning. In the Jewish Orthodox world, Hasidism became stronger and more dominant and even in the non-Hasidic Orthodox world kabbalistic practices and beliefs gained great credence. Legends became historical facts, the supernatural became everyday and the bent toward mysticism was firmly entrenched within Jewish society. As always, in such an environment, charlatans and self-proclaimed gurus also abounded. So-called kabbalists arose and rock stars announced their adherence to Kabbala, its study and its way of life. Superficial reading of *Zohar* substituted for intense study of Torah and Talmud. Palm reading and magic potions reappeared popularly in sections of Jewish society. The mystic dominated the rational amongst many Jews. The complicated difficulties of modern life and society undoubtedly contributed to this trend of thought and behavior. Since the rational world afforded little comfort or ease of mind, many sought refuge in the mysterious and unknown for support and surcease.

Toward the end of the twentieth century, a new burst of messianism surfaced around the person of Rabbi Menaḥem Mendel Schneerson, the Brooklyn-based, seventh Lubavitcher rebbe. There is abundant thought and theory present that he in fact did consider himself messianic material. His followers certainly believed him to be of that caliber. Even after his death many if not most of the members of the Lubavitch movement believed him to be the messiah even though officially the movement took no such public stand. More than a decade after his passing, full page advertisements, signs on Israeli buses and roads and proclamations voiced at the end of prayer services in Lubavitch synagogues the world over still proclaim his messianic quality and role. It is needless again to say that this has caused schism and division and great controversy within the Jewish world. Messianism and its companion ideas of mysticism and other worldliness have always proven to be potentially dangerous and volatile concepts in the Jewish world, subject to misuse and manipulation. Nevertheless, these concepts always reemerge regularly within the patterns of Jewish life and history. Maimonides advised not even discussing the concept, stating that when the messianic era arrives somehow we will know and recognize it. "And even if the Messiah may tarry I will daily await his coming."

Chapter Eight

Technology and Inventions

Technology and man's ingenuity is what has propelled civilization forward over the ages. Over the centuries new inventions and advancing technology has impacted Jewish life as it has generally. Many societies, especially in the Western world have consistently pursued new technologies and products. Other societies have at least initially shunned new emerging technologies and preferred to change more slowly and remain with their traditional ways of life and social behavior. Both groups have been, and are currently still, represented in the Jewish world, though it must be said that Jewish society generally has been in the forefront of adapting new technologies for its use. In fact it is no exaggeration to state that a large proportion of all rabbinic responsa over the millennia deals with issues raised by new technologies and inventions. The rabbis of the Midrash complimented Noah for inventing the plow, a major technological advance of his time. Technological advances have made the daily activities of modern life more comfortable and less strenuous than ever before. The perennial problem is how to fit ever-changing physical circumstances and inventions into the framework of the eternal principles of Jewish law/halakha and values. Moses never dealt with electricity, automobiles or computers, yet the halakhic principles established by Moses on Sinai cover all of these as well. It is within this context that the Jewish approach to new and emerging technologies clearly emerges in the pattern of the ages. The general rule is that Jewish society is pro-technology though it may take time for halakha to fully define and absorb new technology into mainstream Jewish life.

In reality this topic deserves a book all unto itself. It is not my intention therefore in this book on patterns in Jewish history to delve into the details and intricacies of halakhic discussion regarding technologies over the ages. I intend only to use broad brush strokes to illustrate how the importance of new and emerging technologies affected Jewish life over time. It should also be noted that when given the opportunity, Jews have generally been in the forefront of technological creativity over time. Astronomy, medicine, mathematics and other sciences have always been vital areas of Jewish study. Jewish life was always open to new inventions, discoveries and products. The matter can be summed up in a famous discussion quoted in a nineteenth-century rabbinic responsa of the Austro-Hungarian Jewish society. A Hasidic master wrote to Rabbi Tzvi Hirsch Chajes about the discovery of the printing press and later the radio. He maintained that since our teacher Moses and King Solomon were the wisest of all men and they did not have a printing press nor did they feel impelled to create such a tool, the use of the printing press for holy documents should be shunned by the Jewish world as being unnecessary. Rabbi Chajes answered him stating that Moses' and Solomon's wisdom had nothing to do with technology and new inventions and that the Jewish world should adapt and use all new technologies to help spread Torah and Godly values throughout Israel and the world generally.

There is no reason to reject new inventions and discoveries that superseded the knowledge of the world and the science of biblical or Talmudic times. All of the later commentators to the Talmud advised that no one should rely on the medicine or cures mentioned in the Talmud. For millennia, bloodletting was seen as a cure for many ailments. George Washington died not from pneumonia but from the bloodletting performed by his doctors to ostensibly cure his pneumonia. Bloodletting was extremely common amongst Jews till very recent times. It certainly is no longer advocated in modern medical practice and has therefore all but disappeared from current Jewish life and society. Many a modern rabbinic decisor of note has familiarized himself with current medical knowledge and practice in order to answer with wisdom and insight the halakhic questions posed to him in medical areas. Hospitals and medical centers, especially here in Israel, have rabbinic decisors on their staffs to advise them in matters of halakha in complicated instances. Technology has changed the practice of medicine completely over the past number of decades and will probably continue to do so over the coming years. Halakha will constantly adapt itself to new technologies and practices in this field. This has been its pattern over all of the millennia of Jewish history. Jews were famous for being doctors in all ages and locations. All medical knowledge fits under the Torah value of the sanctity of human life and the obligation to preserve, cure and nurture it. Every advance in medical knowledge and treatment of illness is therefore an advance of holiness in the world as well. All sections of Jewish society subscribe to and live by this doctrine in matters of health and medicine. I will discuss these issues regarding the Jewish relationship toward health and medical issues in much more detail in Chapter Twelve.

There have been technological advances that have significantly changed Jewish society and scholarship. Foremost among them, naturally, was the invention of the printing press in the fifteenth century. Though the Church in Europe restricted Jewish ownership of printing presses, and Jewish books had to have the imprimatur of the Church censor, by the sixteenth century Jewish presses (originally ostensibly fronted by Gentiles) existed all over Europe. The nature of printing – is it merely another form of writing or is it a method of engraving – was the subject of much rabbinic responsa. Could printing serve as a means to produce a valid *sefer Torah*, a *get* (bill of divorce) or a mezuza? The accepted opinion over time was that printing could not substitute for the handwritten work of a scribe in these matters. But the printing press was a great boon to Jewish scholarship. The *Shulḥan Arukh* of Rabbi Yosef Caro and the glosses to it of Rabbi Moshe Isserles (Rama), this basic compendium of Jewish law produced in the sixteenth century, would never have been able to gain such quick and almost universal authority and approbation in the Jewish world if not for the almost immediate printing-press production of thousands of its copies. There is a veritable explosion of

Jewish scholarly works occasioned by the fact that the printing press afforded cheap and wide copying and popular distribution. The printing press allowed for the spread of knowledge amongst the masses of Israel. Everyone now could possess the basic books of Jewish life. The history and vicissitudes of printing the Talmud also deserves a book unto itself. Suffice it to say that now with computer printing processes the Talmud has become more accessible to the masses of world Jewry than ever before in its long history. Of course the printing press also produced much undesirable reading material as well. Technology itself is neutral. Nevertheless, in many instances the Jewish world has adopted new technologies for the spread of Torah in spite of the lurking danger of that technology being misused or abused for negative purposes.

In our time the computer and its attendant word processor have also revolutionized Jewish life. There is a wealth of Torah available today on the internet. There is also a lot of malevolent junk present on the internet. In our present time, ignoring the use of the computer is almost an impossibility. Just as the Jews learned to use the printing press wisely and for holy and positive ends and goals, so, too, the use of the computer and the internet will be adjusted and adapted to halakhic standards. No one is going back to use typewriters, carbon paper or mimeograph machines in yeshivot or women's seminaries. Perhaps in no other society is the use of cell phones and personal pagers as widespread as it is in Jewish society the world over. The number of cell phones operating in Israel exceeds the population of the country by at least a million units. In the field of "high-tech" and creative technological invention Israel is one of the world's leaders. It is also a world leader in solar energy, wind power, desalination of sea water and drip irrigation for agriculture. Jews feel that their participation in advancing technology is part of the fulfillment of the Godly promise to Abraham that, through the efforts of his descendants, all of mankind would be blessed and benefited. Technology can heal and destroy, warm and burn, educate and pervert. The struggle therefore of Jews over all of Jewish history is not with technology itself, but rather with how to control and use it for positive purposes and prevent its exploitation for negative purposes. It may be that certain technologies such as television in the eyes of many have become so perverted in their use that they are not salvageable anymore in traditional Jewish society. Yet in Israel there are television channels that promulgate Torah and Jewish knowledge and are very popular. The ability to speak to and teach many thousands of Jews at one time cannot be measured or minimized. Technology and how to handle it in its various ramifications remains a very sensitive and omnipresent issue in Jewish life.

One of the more controversial issues in Jewish history regarding technology and its use was the invention of the matza-baking machine in the middle of the nineteenth century. The machine which greatly simplified the matza-baking process received the approbation of many of the leading rabbinic scholars of the time. However many other rabbis, chiefly Hasidic masters, criticized the innovation on technical halakhic grounds and on the grounds that the women who usually worked in the hand matza-baking bakeries would now lose their income. The rabbis who supported the matza machines answered all of the technical halakhic objections (today's matza-baking machines have dealt with all these concerns and there are probably many more halakhic problems with hand-baked matzot nowadays than with machine-made matzot) and stated that temporary displacement of labor is always a natural byproduct of industrial and technological progress and modernization and cannot be helped. This issue is one of the problems that lie at the heart of the debate as to how much technological advance is enough for us. There is always a trend in human life to return to the "good old days" when seemingly life was simpler and more serene. But all of the pursuit of more and better technology is based on labor-saving principles. I imagine that this debate about technology will still be alive and well centuries from now. In our time, machine matza enjoys the highest degree of kashrut approval and supervision though it is still not used by most Hasidic households and others as well who feel that even though it is certainly kosher, it is not traditional – machine-made matza certainly did not exist in Egypt or Temple times – and Pesaḥ is the holiday of Jewish tradition above all.

Jewish males traditionally wore beards. In the modern era when clean-shaven males were the dictated style, religious Jews began to be clean shaven. They accomplished this by using sulphurous compounds on their face to remove the hair. This method was potentially dangerous –

many a chin was burned in the process – and very malodorous. The invention of the electric shaver, which used a refined method of cutting hair with a scissors action, became the accepted norm in the Jewish world. Though sporting beards has now become more fashionable even in more modern religious circles, today most modern religious Jews are clean-shaven and use an electric shaver to accomplish this look. Every so often, new objections to the use of electric shavers are raised but the overwhelming opinion of the decisors of halakha is to permit their use. Again, the use of technology to meet halakhic standards has allowed Jews opportunities in the modern world that otherwise may not have been present for them.

The creation of the State of Israel and the necessity of operating the state on a continuous basis have raised problems and solutions. The question of the use of electricity generated by Jewish–owned and operated power plants on Shabbat has been a thorny one. The general basic question regarding the nature of electricity as viewed in halakha is over a century old. Originally, many great decisors thought of electricity as fitting under the halakhic definition of fire, and thus, on Holidays, when using fire lit from existing fire (the electricity already in the wire) is permissible, electric lights could be turned on. This opinion found widespread acceptance in the first half of the twentieth century. I remember as a child growing up in Chicago that in many rabbinic houses electric lights were lit on Festival days. However the opinion of Rabbi Avraham Yeshayahu Karelitz (Ḥazon Ish), that electricity was basically the building of a circuit and thus fell under the halakhic category of "building" (*boneh*), became the accepted norm in Jewish life in the latter half of the twentieth century and thus lighting lamps on holidays was forbidden. Many Jews in Israel do not use the government-provided electricity on Shabbat. In Israel this opinion is strongly held in Benei Berak, the dwelling place of Rabbi Karelitz. However the Jews of Jerusalem and of most of Israel do use such electricity on Shabbat (naturally if it was turned on before the advent of Shabbat itself) since such electricity is anyway necessary for hospitals and the non-Jews living in the area. Much of the electricity produced today in Israel on Shabbat is generated automatically without anyone really obligated to operate any machinery unless something goes wrong, thus making it a potentially less serious halakhic issue. The exact nature of electricity as it pertains to Jewish law is still under debate and research. The great Jerusalem sage of the last half of the twentieth century, Rabbi Shlomo Zalman Auerbach, wrote extensively on the subject and disagreed with Rabbi Karelitz as to the basic nature of electricity in its application to halakhic decisions. Physicists themselves have yet to determine the nature of electricity – wave, streams, purely molecular – and thus eventual clarity regarding this matter as far as Jewish law is concerned is still a way distant. But as is well known in general society, law always lags behind technological achievement.

Among the technological innovations that now exist in Jewish life are Shabbat clocks and timers which control lighting, heating, air conditioning and other electrical connections. Though again there is some rabbinic opinion opposing such controls, they are nevertheless currently ubiquitous and widely accepted in Jewish society. There have been important innovations in computerized technology that have now allowed for reputable rabbinic endorsements for Shabbat elevators/lifts, escalators, moving walkways, mobile self-propelled wheelchairs and even electric automobiles and security vehicles. Though there will understandably be objection to such devices as not being within the traditional spirit of Shabbat rest, there is no doubt that continued advances in technology will result in more and more devices such as these, which are in conformity with Halakha, becoming part of religious Jewish Shabbat life. There are now Shabbat refrigerators, stoves, warmers, and ovens, all available from leading appliance manufacturers that are gaining popularity for use in Jewish households. Technology has revolutionized the production of food products and has greatly aided in maintaining the high standards and wide distribution of kosher food products throughout the world. The pattern of Jewish history has always been that every great technological breakthrough and invention has eventually been incorporated within and adapted to Jewish life and halakhic standards. We are not like the Amish in shunning modern technological achievements, nor are Jews anti-technology in any fashion. Not all gadgets and appliances spawned by modern technology can be deemed necessary for improving Jewish life and somehow aiding spiritual growth. But technology as a whole and as a given fact in the progress of civilization in human development is seen as a positive factor in Jewish tradition and everyday life. Today,

Torah can be downloaded from the internet, heard on automobile CD players, viewed as DVDs, shared by e-mails, published by desktops and appear on one's hand-held smartphones. The explosion of communication occasioned by the advances in technology has made Torah accessible to the masses of Israel in a way and in numbers hardly ever even imagined before. Thus technology again becomes, as with the invention of the printing press, the great ally of Torah study and its dissemination throughout the world. The progress of technology and its use in Torah study and Jewish life is in itself another expression of the eternity and timelessness of Torah.

Chapter Nine

Customs and Traditions

All societies survive through the retention of customs and traditions. If ritual law, halakha and Torah observance are the keystones of Jewish existence, the customs and traditions of Israel are the chain that has kept Israel bound to the Torah and its laws and values. The rabbis called the customs and traditions of Israel "the lessons of your mother" – in contrast and at the same time complementing "the teachings and disciplines of your father." Discipline and teachings are sometimes cold, harsh, demanding. Your mother's lessons are warm, loving, comfortable and reassuring. Thus the relationship of the Jewish people to customs and traditions is a millennia-long romance. Infused with holy memories and meaningful vignettes and life's wisdoms, customs and traditions have long been a dominant factor in Jewish life. Customs and their strengths are already acknowledged in the Talmud, specifically in the Jerusalem Talmud. This gave birth to a very flexible and potentially dangerous concept that custom can sometimes even overrule Halakha. In order to prevent this idea from gaining public credence and practical application, we find that throughout the ages, the great sages of Israel have always attempted to minimize the instances of custom overriding simple halakha. In the eighth century, the leader of Babylonian Jewry,

Rabbi Yehudai Gaon, wrote to the small Jewish community still living in the land of Israel that their customs contravened Halakha. The Israelis answered him in the usual pugnacious manner of Israelis that custom supersedes halakha and that they fully intended to continue to observe their customs no matter what the Babylonian sage had to say about them.

Customs evolve and many times are influenced by unknown and even non-Jewish sources. A people does not live in Spain for eight hundred years without becoming at least slightly Spanish in its customs and mores. The same is certainly true for central and eastern Europe (Germany, Italy, Poland, Russia, Lithuania, Hungary, Bohemia, Romania, Austria, etc.) Many customs that the Jews adopted in their long exile were not necessarily of Jewish origin. Yet over the ages, all customs that entered Jewish life, no matter what their original source may have been, were invested with authority and holiness – many times over the objections of the rabbis and sages of the time. Customs had such a strong hold on Jewish behavior and lifestyle that Rabbi Yaakov Emden (eighteenth century) ruefully remarked that it was regrettable that the commandment not to steal was written in the Torah and was not a custom, for had it been a custom it would have wider acceptance and practice amongst the Jewish people. Thus the struggle between custom and Halakha, between the sages of Israel and its masses, was and is a never-ending contest, and Jewish history attests that custom usually wins out. The rabbis were willing to grant that custom takes precedence in monetary and commercial affairs, stating in essence that agreed-upon business custom is essentially halakha itself in that realm of human activity. However the main disputes concerned custom in ritual matters and prayer, Holiday and Shabbat laws, and the extent of rabbinic authority over the community and the masses.

An accepted principle that was adopted even in Talmudic times was that when there is considerable doubt and much dispute as to what the halakha actually is, the customs of the people in this matter will prevail. However, there were sages who stated that the customs that one should follow are only those that are stricter than the apparent halakha, but customs that introduce leniencies that the halakha did not countenance should be discarded. This is apparently the opinion of Rabbi Yaakov ben Me'ir (Rabbeinu Tam), the twelfth-century grandson of Rashi and the head of the school of the Tosafists. He wrote regarding a lenient custom opposed to a ruling of Rashi in the matter of kashrut of animal lungs that have a certain type of lesion upon them, that the letters of *minhag* – custom – are the same as those of *Gehenom* – Hell! However, both from the Talmud itself and from later works of the sages of Israel, it seems that customs that were essentially more lenient than the original halakha also had validity. Apparently this was in line with a Talmudic concept that there are times when the halakha itself is set as such and such, but nevertheless we do not teach it or follow it publicly. This flexibility relative to halakha and some of its decisions created the loophole through which custom marched and took hold in the Jewish world.

The upshot of all of this was that a certain consensus was reached regarding the relationship of custom and Halakha. It may generally be stated that the consensus included the following rules: (1) When there was doubt as to what the actual original halakha is, then the custom will decide the matter; (2) when the matter does not really touch upon behavior that is forbidden or permitted, such as matters of blessings and prayer texts, then the custom even if not sanctioned by the prevailing rabbinic authorities is allowed to continue; (3) custom cannot prevail over established halakha in matters of Torah or Talmudic ritual law as to what is forbidden or permitted; and (4) when a major dispute exists among the halakhic authorities as to what the halakha should be, the custom of the community or even the individual is valid.

In the later Middle Ages and early modern period, when the study of *Zohar* and Kabbala spread throughout the Jewish world, many new kabbalistic customs entered Jewish life. Even those sages who opposed the widespread study of Kabbala amongst the masses, nevertheless adopted kabbalistic customs in their communities. Naturally this was not without dissension and division within those communities. Even so, kabbalistic customs were widespread throughout Sephardic and Ashkenazic Jewry. Both Rabbi Yosef Caro in his *Shulḥan Arukh* and Rabbi Moshe Isserles in his "tablecloth" (*Mapa*) glosses to the *Shulḥan Arukh* included many customs, kabbalistic and non-kabbalistic as well, in their monumental and authoritative works. Thus custom itself was enshrined in the major halakhic works that have ruled Jewish life ever since the sixteenth century. Rabbi Shmuel HaLevi, the seventeenth-century author of *Naḥalat Shiva,* a well-known halakhic work, attacked the concept of custom overruling halakha but apparently to little avail. The rise of the eighteenth-century Hasidic movement, with its heavy emphasis on kabbalistic thought and mass practice, created many customs that were enshrined as obligatory behavior within the various Hasidic groups adopting these differing customs. Some customs such as the wearing of a ritual belt (*gartel*) during prayer services and other occasions became universal Hasidic custom as did the change from strictly Ashkenazic ritual text of prayer to one that resembled Sephardic text. Amongst the Lithuanian Jews, many private customs of Rabbi Eliyahu ben Shlomo Zalman, the Gaon of Vilna, took public hold and were observed in their synagogues and yeshivot. Some of those customs have become the accepted norm in today's Jerusalem as well.

Even as late as the nineteenth century there were great rabbinic authorities who opposed the custom of *kaparot* – the slaughter of chickens before Yom Kippur as being an expiation of one's sins. In Lithuanian Jewry the superstitious custom was modified to giving coins to charity instead of slaughtering chickens. Nevertheless, the custom has persisted and even gained strength and followers especially in the Hasidic society, and the custom of *kaparot* with chickens is alive and well (though not for the chickens) in present-day Jerusalem even within the "Lithuanian" society. The line between custom and superstition is a very thin one and has often been crossed in Jewish history. In our world, the custom of wearing red strings to ward off the evil eye is quite prevalent. The origin of that custom is clearly not Jewish, it being part of Italian and Sicilian lore. Nevertheless it is certainly present in today's Jewish society.

Perhaps the strongest and longest-lasting custom that has become a part of Ashkenazic Jewish life is that of the non-use of *kitniyot** on Pesaḥ. This custom, which originated in the early Middle Ages, was apparently based upon the use of legumes to make a type of Pesaḥ bread. The banning of the use of legumes stemmed from the confusion that might arise

* *Kitniyot* refers to certain grains, legumes and their derivatives which are customarily not owned, eaten or benefited from on Pesaḥ because of their similarity to *ḥametz* (which is forbidden on Pesaḥ) in their appearance, harvesting and processing methods, and due to the possibility of having *ḥametz* mixed with them.

from people thinking that if bread made from rice, beans, peas, etc. was permissible, then bread made from oats, barley, rye, wheat and spelt was also somehow acceptable – these latter grains being pure *ḥametz* if not carefully and expeditiously turned into quick-baked matza. This custom is a very strong one and the rabbis over the ages have been very loath to relax its severity even in seemingly extraordinary circumstances. In fact the custom has expanded in our time to even include liquids derived from legumes and other such legume derivatives. The Sephardic world generally does not observe this custom of *kitniyot* though there are some Sephardic communities that do not use rice on Pesaḥ. In our time, American corn, which was unknown to Europe and the Middle East until the eighteenth century, is also treated as being *kitniyot*. However, tea, coffee, sugar, garlic, cocoa, tobacco and other like ingredients are not considered to be *kitniyot*, though all of them were at one time or another discussed in rabbinic literature as perhaps being such. Amongst the masses, the custom to include garlic as being *kitniyot* was widespread even when rabbinic decision was almost unanimous that it not be considered so. The whole subject of *kitniyot* is one area where custom completely rules. The fact that the entire matter of *kitniyot* is absent from Sephardic Jewish communities only emphasizes the role of differing customs in different Jewish communities. Rabbinic wisdom decreed that instead of arguing over the efficacy of one custom over another differing one, each community should observe its customs and traditions. In cases of "mixed" marriages between Sephardim and Ashkenazim, in the absence of agreement among the spouses as to which customs will prevail in the house, the usual practice is that the custom of the husband takes precedence.

Another contentious custom that exists in the Ashkenazic world regarding Pesaḥ is that of the non-use of matza-meal flour on Pesaḥ in conjunction with cooking and baking. This matter called "*gebrokts*" (literally, ground or broken matza) was not widespread until the rise of Hasidism in eighteenth- and nineteenth-century eastern Europe. The non-Hasidic Lithuanian Jewish world never adopted this custom and even the Hasidic world allows *gebrokts* on the eighth day of Pesaḥ in the Diaspora. This custom apparently arose from the chance that the matza would not be baked thoroughly enough and thus a kernel of grain would remain embedded in the matza. When the matza was made wet in cooking, baking or dipping, that kernel would begin to ferment and could become *ḥametz*. Since the prohibition against *ḥametz* on Pesaḥ applies even to the minutest amount of grain, this custom took hold in the Hasidic world and is observed by most Jews of eastern European background even today. Those Jews of Lithuanian descent do not observe the custom of *gebrokts* and this often leads to a certain disconnect within families where the generations of eastern European Jews of these different customs have married each other and the question arises as to who eats or does not eat matza balls and the like at the same meal. There is nothing quite like being Jewish when matters of custom are involved. To the outsider the issues may appear to be slightly amusing. However, in my rabbinic experience, I have witnessed that unfortunately these matters are deadly serious to those involved and can tear family bonds asunder. Therefore, even observance of custom requires good sense, tolerance and prioritizing values.

There is one area of Jewish law and life which is almost completely governed by custom and that is the subject of *avelut* – the procedures of grieving, mourning and consoling the bereaved. Since we are dealing with the dreaded unknown, death itself, it is understandable that custom should have a strong hold on the matter. Kabbalistic customs rule in these areas. For instance the covering of mirrors in the house of the mourner is a custom that has acquired almost universal acceptance, even in homes that sadly do not otherwise observe basic Jewish law and practice. Death is spooky and when it comes to spooks even the most hardened rational intellect wavers. Visiting graves, placing stones on the monuments, reciting *kaddish* in memory or in honor of the dead, the *Yizkor* service held four times in the year in the midst of Holiday prayer services, lighting *yahrzeit* lamps or candles to mark the anniversary of the death of a family member and other such death-related customs connected to grief and consolation are all fairly late arrivals into Jewish life, mostly unmentioned in records of biblical and Talmudic times. Much has been written lately about the Jewish way of grieving and consolation, mostly based on the customs that now prevail. Most of these customs have been hallowed into becoming Jewish law and halakha itself, and occupy great space and discussion in rabbinic writings and scholarly works. Jewish law discourages undue mourning over death. It is the way of God's world. The customs of Israel in these matters are meant to ease the mourner back into normal life and routine and somehow begin to assuage the pain of the loss and death of a loved one.

In general one may maintain that wherever the original halakha appeared to be sparse, custom rushed in to fill the void and establish the norm of behavior in Jewish life. Nowhere in Jewish life is this more evident than in the customs relating to death, burial and mourning. In a broader sense one may see that tradition and customs have eased the terrible exile for Israel and helped us preserve our faith and family structure against overwhelmingly difficult odds. Differing wedding customs amongst the ethnic groupings of Jews the world over (though the halakhic requirements of the ceremony are universal) are testimony to this truism. This is also apparent in the ironclad "custom of our fathers that remains in our hands" to observe a second day of Holiday on Pesaḥ, Shavuot and Sukkot in the Diaspora. This observance was originally a matter of halakha since there was real doubt as to which day was exactly the correct date of the Holiday. However, with the establishment and acceptance of the calculations of the permanent Jewish calendar after the demise of the Sanhedrin in the fifth century, the doubts regarding the exact date of the Holiday were seemingly removed. But the second day of the Diaspora Holidays then morphed from absolute halakha into custom. And the custom became as binding as the halakha itself had been. It was the "extra" day of the Holidays that helped the Jewish people survive the long exile. Those movements that did away with the custom of the "second" day of the Holiday soon found that their adherents had now lost observance of the "first" day of the Holidays as well. The reformers and progressives amongst us have constantly underestimated the power of custom in the life of a society and a people, certainly in Jewish society and the people of Israel. The warmth and love of our mothers as represented by the customs and traditions of Israel are the mainstays of Jewish life even now in our land of Israel and its Jewish state and in a more favorable Diaspora atmosphere. Jewish free thinkers and agnostics have mocked Jewish customs in every age and country of Jewish residence. Yet they have been unable to find any worthwhile substitute for the tradition and customs so much maligned by them, any other mechanism that would help ensure Jewish continuity and survival. Is it not perhaps that all of us have only one mother? And the one mother of Israel in this matter remains our sense of tradition and the customs developed over the ages to protect the Torah and enrich Jewish life.

Chapter Ten

Anti-Semitism and Persecution

The term "anti-Semitism" is a nineteenth-century creation. It describes hatred of Jews. I use it in this chapter to describe anti-Jewish ideas and behavior throughout the ages, even in the times when this elegant euphemism for irrational hatred did not yet exist. The brutal truth is that as long as there have been Jews in the world there have also been those who have hated them, whether for imagined cause or simply as a manifestation of all-too-common irrational human behavior.

The Jew has always been the eternal "other" in general society. One of the great sages of the Mishna stated that it is halakha – a given immutable law – that Esau hates Jacob. Jews therefore have always been the ultimate outsider. It also seems fairly obvious that Heaven allows anti-Semitism as a weapon against complete Jewish assimilation into the non-Jewish world. The sad story begins with our father Abraham. The Midrash states that he was called "*haIvri*," the root of which connotes both "the Hebrew" and "the one from the other side," and that fact extends through the next four millennia of human history. However, there are different rationales for this hateful behavior and there are patterns of intensification and relaxation of it throughout our history. In the biblical period, Abraham was accorded a grudging respect by the rulers of the lands of the Fertile Crescent (the great kings involved in the decades-long war during Abraham's lifetime), as well as Abimelech, the King of the Philistines. Abraham was called a "prince of God who dwells in our midst," and by the end of his life had acquired wealth, position and tranquility amongst his heathen neighbors. He was also very successful in spreading the message of monotheism and goodness toward other humans to his society. Rabbi Menaḥem HaMe'iri, (fourteenth-century Provencal sage) states that Abraham's influence and ideas captivated over half of the people living in his society during his lifetime. His son Isaac, however, suffered persecution from the Philistines who destroyed his wells and contested his attempts to dig new ones. The Torah offers no reason as to why the Philistines should have so behaved, especially as the destruction of the wells was counterproductive to their own economic interests. It represents the classic case that is repeated in anti-Semitic acts throughout the ages: I care less about what I have than what I do not want you to have. But eventually Abimelech, the King of the Philistines, strikes a pact of accommodation with Isaac, and the Torah does not record for us any further conflicts with or persecution of Isaac during his long lifetime.

In the next generation, Jacob suffers persecution from his brother Esau, his father-in-law, Laban, and from Shechem and Hamor who combine to allow the rape of his daughter, Dina. We read that Jacob and his sons engaged in wars with neighboring tribes. When Jacob's son Joseph saves Egypt from a disastrous famine, Egypt rewards this life-saving behavior by enslaving their descendants. There arises a Pharaoh who knows not of Joseph. Jews have often disproportionately built up the country that they have resided in only to have their achievements resented by the very citizenry that benefited from them. The story of Egypt is tragically a recurring pattern in Jewish history. After the exodus from Egypt, the Jews fight a number of wars against enemy tribes in the desert of Sinai. These wars are not necessarily classic anti-Semitism as much as they are wars over territory and national goals of conflicting societies. In fact throughout the entire biblical period, culminating with the destruction of the First Temple and the Babylonian Exile, the wars fought by Israel and Judah against external enemies have less to do with religion as they do with national and territorial causes. These were struggles regarding empire, wealth and territorial borders. Jewish monotheism was unique among the beliefs of the ancient world but that difference – major and defining as it was – did not spark anti-Semitic feeling. As long as Jews had a national home in the land of Israel, an independent monarchy and national interests consistent with those of other nations, anti-Semitism, as it became known in later times, does not seem to have played a major role in Jewish life.

All of this changed for Jews with the destruction of the First Temple and the exile of Jews into a foreign and often hostile Diaspora. Jews who were exiled into Babylonia and Persia attempted to assimilate into the general population and were rebuffed. In Persia, Haman arose and prescribed genocide as the solution to the nascent Jewish "problem." In a foreign society, now living outside of the land of Israel and no longer having any national identity of their own, Jews were different, exceptional, and raised suspicions as to their loyalty and their ability to be integrated into the general society. When Ezra led the return of Jews to the land of Israel, most of the Jews remained in the Diaspora, thus establishing the pattern of Jews living everywhere in the known world and always being a minority in population and in matters of custom, religion and lifestyle. Thus was the image of the Jew as the eternal outsider established and confirmed. Being the outsider always provoked enmity, suspicion, and persecution from those who were the insiders. The Greek imperialists could not accept the resistance of Jews to paganism and to Greek culture and sexual attitudes. The victory of the Hasmoneans over the Syrian Greeks – the story of Ḥanukka – only hardened Greek enmity to Jews and Judaism. Anti-Jewish tracts circulated in the Greek world. When Rome replaced Greece as the dominant force in the civilized world it inherited much of Greek anti-Semitism. The fierce, armed Jewish resistance to Roman rule culminating in the destruction of the Second Temple in 70 CE only hardened Roman dislike of the Jews. Nevertheless, a thriving and influential Jewish community existed in Rome itself and Jews accompanied the march of Roman legions throughout Europe establishing small Jewish enclaves that later developed into major Jewish centers of life and learning.

It was the rise of Christianity in the early centuries of the Common Era that created the base of religious anti-Semitism that was to dominate Jewish-Gentile relations for millennia. Christianity simply could not accept the continued Jewish rejection of Jesus and Christian theology and practice. The early Church fathers were fiercely and vociferously anti-Jewish, piling invective and false accusations against Jews and Judaism in their teachings and writings. In many cities in Libya and Egypt, Jews fought violent pitched battles against the Christian and Greek communities with heavy loss of life on all sides. Anti-Semitic tracts were written by Greek and Roman scholars with all of the accusations that would persist throughout the ages already trotted out as being factual. The Church would later incorporate these false accusations into its anti-Jewish agenda and teachings. Jewish scholars such as Philo of Alexandria and others responded by writing detailed works refuting all of these false accusations and nonsensical indictments. But the poison had already spread throughout the classical world. So when Constantine turned the Roman Empire into a Christian one the persecution of Jews increased. It now became not only a national hatred but a religiously sanctioned one as well.

In the fourth century, the Council of Nicaea decided doctrine that was heavily anti-Jewish, and its minutes accused the Jews of deicide, judging them to be eternally damned. The Byzantine Eastern Church persecuted the Jews unmercifully and, under this situation, the Jewish community of the land of Israel was practically destroyed in the fifth century. The Roman Catholic Church also discriminated and persecuted the Jewish populations living under its domain. As Europe plunged into the Dark Ages, Jewish life in much of Europe was crippled by anti-Jewish decrees. The tribes who conquered and dismembered the Roman Empire in the fifth century became Christianized themselves. They inherited both the Roman and Christian strains of anti-Semitism and made them the basis of their behavior and attitude toward Jews and Judaism. It is no exaggeration to note that Jewish life throughout the Mediterranean basin was seriously threatened with extinction during this period of rapid Christianization of Europe and parts of the Middle East. Ironically, it would be the rise of the new faith of Islam in the seventh century that would thwart the genocidal plans of the Byzantine

Church and provide the Jewish world some relief from the increasingly violent anti-Semitism of the Christian world.

Mohammed and the Koran took on an ambivalent attitude toward Jews and Judaism. Mohammed was evidently originally convinced that the Jews would willingly accept his new religion since it was purely monotheistic and included the great Jewish biblical figures in its pantheon of prophets and spiritual leaders. In places, the Koran has very complimentary statements about Jews and their faith. However, once the Jews rejected Mohammed as a prophet and with him the truth of the Mohammedan faith, Mohammed and the Koran turned bitterly anti-Jewish. Jews were nevertheless allowed *dhimmi* – decidedly second class – status in Muslim society and there was always a certain flexibility in Muslim treatment of the Jews depending on place, time and circumstance. The Muslims swept the Byzantines out of the Middle East and successfully invaded and conquered most of the Iberian Peninsula. The Jews followed in the wake of the conquering Muslim armies and soon established themselves as an integral part of the overall Muslim society in North Africa and Iberia. Particularly in Spain, the Jews rose to great official and economic heights in the early Middle Ages, and thus Jews enjoyed a "golden age" in Spain under Muslim rule for almost four centuries. Muslim Spain boasted of Jewish prime ministers, generals, ministers of the treasury, poets, linguists and diplomats. The exigencies of the time and the struggle against the common Christian enemy in Catalonia papered over any major religious disagreements between the Jews and the Muslim ruling class. But hatred and resentment of the Jews in Spain simmered just below the surface of the masses of Muslim society. Sporadic pogroms against Jews and Jewish leaders took place in the eighth and ninth centuries. The Jews had made the fatal error of being too successful in Muslim Spain. This error would resurface again as a continuing pattern in Jewish history.

In the twelfth century, a fanatical Muslim group, the Almohads, overthrew the reigning Muslim authorities and then ruled Spain and Morocco for over seventy years. Under their rule the Jews suffered greatly. Pogroms, exile, and forced conversions to Islam were regular occurrences. Even after the fall of the Almohads, Jewish Spain never recovered its former position or glory. The Christian kings of the north began the slow process of reconquering Iberia from Muslim hands and control. With them came the fierce anti-Semitism of the Church and Christian Europe. This anti-Semitism, open, brazen and religiously and governmentally sanctioned, culminated in a great nationwide pogrom in 1391 when thousands of Jews were killed or forcibly converted to Christianity. The entire sad story of Iberian Jewry ended in 1492, when the Jews of Spain were exiled or forcibly converted to Christianity, and in 1496, when the same fate befell the Jews of Portugal. The Church had set up the Holy Office of the Inquisition to make certain that the Jewish Conversos truly accepted Christianity. Many Jews were arrested, tortured and executed by this hateful organization of religious bigotry and violent hatred. As late as the nineteenth century the Inquisition still operated in Latin and Central America. The anti-Semites are always looking to find and destroy the last Jew on earth.

The Ashkenazic Jewish community in France and the Rhineland enjoyed a period of tranquility in the ninth and tenth centuries. Jewish communities flourished in Mainz, Speyer, Worms, Troyes, Orleans, Lyon and even Paris. However the First Crusade in 1096 unleashed a pogrom that destroyed many of these major Jewish communities. The later failed Crusades only intensified this anti-Jewish behavior. Jews were the Christ killers and were not to be tolerated in Christian society. The "blood libel" that accused Jews of somehow using the blood of Christian children in their baking of Pesaḥ matzot was created in the thirteenth century in England and has survived in world society from those times till today. By Church edict, Jews were forced to wear a yellow star on their clothing and special ridiculous "Jew hats" were made part of coerced Jewish dress. In the thirteenth century the Jews of England and France were expelled and Jewish books were publicly burned. In the fourteenth century the Black Death caused by the bubonic plague ravaged Europe killing one third of its population. Christian Europe, looking for a scapegoat on which to blame this tragedy, naturally targeted the Jews. The Jews were accused of poisoning the wells and causing the plague. Terrible pogroms occurred in Germany, Bohemia, Austria and Provence and the Jews were driven eastward in Europe to find safe haven. The kings of Poland invited the Jews to immigrate to their kingdoms to build up the country economically and socially. From the fourteenth century onwards, Jews were an integral part of Poland, Lithuania, Volhynia and Belarus. The long story of eastern European Jewry, lasting over seven centuries, is one of promising beginnings and a disastrous tragic conclusion. Jews also remained settled in parts of Germany, Austria, Bohemia and eventually (especially beginning in the sixteenth century) in the Balkan countries, Hungary, Romania and Greece. The remnants of Spanish Jewry settled in Turkey and throughout the Mediterranean basin. Some also came to Germany and eastern Europe where their traditions became more Ashkenazi.

The sixteenth-century Protestant Reformation and the ensuing Thirty Year War between Catholics and Protestants turned into a blood bath for the Jews of central Europe. Martin Luther, like Mohammed before him, somehow believed that his new religion, a reformed brand of Christianity, would appeal to Jews and allow them to convert to his take on the Christian faith. When this did not happen he turned his venomous pen against the Jews. He wrote terrible diatribes against the Jews and Judaism and much of his hatred-laden statements were adopted by later anti-Semites. Thus no matter which side won, so to speak, in the schismatic wars within Christianity, the Jews would always certainly be the losers. The Jewish response to all of this was always low-key and submissive. They would try to ride out the storm. In spite of the more liberating influences of the Renaissance in papal Italy, a ghetto was established in Venice in the sixteenth century confining Jews to a certain area in the city. This model was soon adopted by the ruling classes throughout Christian Europe. Even when not forced to, Jews soon willingly took to life within their own self-made ghetto for security, social and religious reasons. In eastern Europe, Jews settled in the *shtetl* – small rural villages, usually containing a few hundred families, the majority of whom were Jewish. The Middle Ages were a terrible time for the Jews of Europe. The installation and canonization of anti-Semitism as part of Church doctrine and attitude was lethal to Jewish hopes for an easier life in the exile. The Jews chafed under these conditions but could by themselves provide no solution to this Jewish "problem." They waited for some sort of divine deliverance from their woes and troubles.

In 1648 a horrific pogrom occurred in Ukraine, Poland, Belarus and Lithuania. It claimed many thousands of Jewish lives and dislocated a quarter of a million Jewish residents of those areas. Sparked by the ambitions of Bogdan Chmielnicki, a Cossack soldier of fortune, to free the Ukrainians from Polish landlord rule, this pogrom marked the beginning of the three-century slide of eastern European Jewry into oblivion. The damage of the pogrom was compounded psychologically and spiritually by the apostasy of Shabbetai Tzvi, the false messiah, immediately in the next decade. Reeling from these blows, the Jewish world now entered the early stages of the Modern Era looking for a way to counter the deadly anti-Semitism that surrounded it. The eighteenth-century ideas of the Enlightenment swept Europe and with these ideas the concepts of tolerance of religions and of the growth of science, agnosticism and democratic government allowed many German, Hungarian, Bohemian and Austrian Jews to escape from the ghetto and eventually achieve legal status. None of these ideas changed Czarist policies of repression against the Jews of Poland, Lithuania, Belarus and Russia. But the influence of the Enlightenment on the Jews of Germany was enormous, eventually leading to the rise of Reform and the assimilation, if not even the conversion to Christianity of hundreds of thousands of Jews. Though officially anti-Semitism was no longer government policy, numerous restrictions on Jews in professions, educational opportunities and commerce still remained. The Jews responded by attempting to become more assimilated and German. The response of German society was to become more anti-Semitic though perhaps not as yet visibly so. Everyone should read Amos Elon's wonderful and chilling book *The Pity of It All,* and gain a picture of how this assimilation of German Jewry led directly to the tragedy of Hitler over a century later. Jews seeped back into England in the eighteenth century but were subject to bitter though usually latent anti-Semitism and discrimination. This was especially reflected in the class-conscious attitudes of English society and so English Jewry assumed a very low profile. Anti-Semitism was, and unfortunately still is, baked into the soul of Gentile Europe. It needs very little to happen to allow it to erupt in murderous fury.

The United States, having freed itself from English colonial administration and rule, proclaimed a bill of rights and religious freedom for all. There were very few Jews in the United States during colonial and Revolutionary War times – probably only about a thousand out of an American-European population of about two million. Nevertheless Jews rose rapidly in commerce, politics and even in the military and navy. In the 1840s there was a sizable immigration of German Reform Jews to the United States. These Jews were subjected to a societal anti-Semitism but nevertheless succeeded amazingly in commerce (Wall Street and retailing) and politics. These Jews, in order to become more American and shatter the glass ceiling that latent anti-Semitism presented, encouraged radical assimilation of American Jewry into its overwhelmingly Christian milieu. With the arrival of millions of eastern European Jews and religious Orthodoxy in nineteenth-century America, anti-Semitism became more open in American social and political life. Nativist, anti-immigration groups made life uncomfortable for many Jews and the friction between ethnic groups all struggling to get ahead in America also sparked many anti-Semitic incidents. But on the whole, America was a minor paradise for Jews compared to the government-backed anti-Semitic atrocities of the Czarist Russian Empire. Jews in America faced discrimination in higher education, corporate structures, restrictive clauses in real estate transactions and in myriad other small things in American life. American Jewry through its B'nai B'rith organization established the Anti-Defamation League to combat anti-Semitism, and later all forms of bigotry and discrimination against any minority, in American society. Before World War II there were openly anti-Semitic parties in America that garnered millions of votes in general elections. However, by the latter half of the twentieth century, almost all of the tacit restrictions against Jewish participation in American commerce, sports, lodging, higher education and politics fell away and American Jews felt that they could be openly Jewish without penalty or fear. Anti-Semitism still existed in America but it was relegated to the basically lunatic fringes of the extreme Left and the neo-Nazi Right in American society.

The anti-Semitism of the Czars in the nineteenth century led them to a drastic policy of anti-Jewish measures. The Czars' hatred of Jews was religiously based, Russian Orthodoxy being far more openly anti-Semitic than even the Roman Catholic Church. Yet, when Theodor Herzl attempted to interest the Pope in the idea of Zionism in order to alleviate the plight of Russian Jewry, the Pope told him that the solution to the "Jewish problem" was the conversion of all Jews to Roman Catholicism. The Czars' agenda for the solution of the "Jewish problem" was "one-third assimilation [conversion to the Russian Orthodox Church] one-third extermination [unceasing waves of pogroms] and one-third emigration from the country." In spite of this draconian governmental policy, the Jewish population in Poland, Lithuania, Belarus and Ukraine (all under the rule of the Czar) actually increased in the nineteenth century! The forcible conscription of Jewish boys into the Russian army for twenty-five-year service terms, the onerous and discriminatory taxation system enforced against Jews and the confinement of Jews within the Pale of Settlement (a 150-mile-wide swath of poor land in the western part of the Russian Empire) made life miserable for Jews living under Czarist rule. This governmental persecution radicalized much of Jewish youth in eastern Europe and Jews were disproportionately represented in the radical groups attempting to assassinate the Czar and bring more democratic rule to Russia. This in turn forced the Czars to blame all of the failings of their miserable administrations on the *zhids* and unleash popularly supported mass pogroms on the hapless Jews living in the Pale of Settlement. The massacre of Jews in Kishinev at the beginning of the twentieth century brought severe condemnation upon the Czar and his government but he did not waver in his anti-Semitic policies. Russian Jewry therefore turned very anti-Czarist and, in the revolutions of 1905 and 1917, Jews were in the forefront of revolutionary activity. A large section of eastern European Jewry became Marxist, and Lenin's politburo contained many Jews who had now become dedicated Bolsheviks and were in essence the new anti-Semites from within the Jewish society itself. The Jewish section of the Communist Party in Russia destroyed Jewish infrastructure and religious life with a vengeance that bordered on hysteria. In the minds of many, Jews became identified with the radical, revolutionary Marxist Left. At the very same time, Jews remained identified with commerce, capitalism, Wall Street and rapacious banking and lending methods and programs. After the emergence of the State of Israel and its refusal to become a Soviet satellite, Stalin turned his latent anti-Semitism into a practical plan to destroy the Jews of Russia, exiling all of them (!) to the Gulag to expire there. Only his death in 1953 aborted this second Holocaust. In short, both the Right and the Left were easily susceptible to becoming virulently anti-Semitic. Thus the Jews were trapped in a classic no-win situation.

The emergence of Charles Darwin's theories of evolution gave birth, undoubtedly unintentionally but nevertheless perniciously, to the theories of social Darwinism. The idea of the survival of the fittest was now to be implemented on the human world. Thus "superior" races were created and "inferior" races were to be assigned their places of servitude in the human scheme of things. Stewart Chamberlain and other crackpot pseudo-scientists created the discipline of eugenics, which would eventually cause untold tragedy and justified murder of innocents on the basis of Darwin's theory of natural selection. Jews were naturally deemed to be an "inferior" race. But since Jews were somehow disproportionately successful in all fields of human endeavor in the nineteenth century, they were regarded as a most dangerous "inferior" race. Anti-Semitism now morphed into a racial defect, no longer just a matter of differing and competing faiths. Religious anti-Semitism was curable by conversion to Christianity or Islam. Racial anti-Semitism had no cure at all. It was a genetic defect that had to be excised by eliminating the carriers of that gene. This racial anti-Semitism became the basis of Hitler's mad ideas of racial purity and led directly to the horrors of the Holocaust. Jews were a bacteria that infected all of human society and therefore had to be eradicated. This form of anti-Semitism became widely accepted in Europe in the nineteenth and twentieth centuries and it accounts for the brutality and heartlessness of so many in perpetrating the Holocaust. Jews were not human beings; they were a pestilence that had to be destroyed.

In the twenty-year period between the two great world wars of the twentieth century, openly anti-Semitic political parties ruled in Lithuania, Poland, Romania and Hungary. Jews were beaten on the streets and subjected to many forms of discrimination and humiliation. Of course all of this would be dwarfed by the ascent of Hitler and Nazism to power in the 1930s. "Jews are our misfortune" became the slogan of Germany and it was echoed all over Europe. The Socialist Jewish prime minister of France in the 1930s, Leon Blum, was hounded by mobs who proclaimed, "Better Hitler than Blum." They soon had their wish fulfilled. The German American Bund openly supported Hitler and conducted mass parades on his behalf in a number of American cities. Stringent immigration quotas meant to exclude Jews from entering the

United States were adopted in the 1920s and were enforced even in the midst of the Holocaust. The head of the State Department's visa section, Breckinridge Long, was a virulent anti-Semite who did everything within his considerable powers to prevent Jews from entering the United States. The powerful Hollywood film, *Gentlemen's Agreement,* produced in the early period after the Second World War highlighted the continuing discrimination against Jews in all walks of American life. But the horrors of the Holocaust, recorded on film and by eyewitnesses, drove overt European and American anti-Semitism underground and made it temporarily unfashionable in the early years after the Second World War. Jews shouted "Never Again!" knowing full well that "again" was somehow yet a distinct possibility. Even so, the Jews asserted themselves strongly in the fight against bigotry and anti-Semitism and attempted to exert their political and commercial influence to combat this hydra-headed scourge.

The story of the Holocaust has been described and detailed in many works and need not be repeated here. The record of the non-German world in the Holocaust was pretty dismal, albeit with private personal exceptions of heroic and noble individuals who risked all to save Jews. The Germans had willing allies in all of the countries that they occupied that were ready to help in the "Final Solution" of the Jewish problem. The French police and Vichy government sent 72,000 French Jews to their deaths in Auschwitz, with the French National Railway System sending the transportation bill to Berlin for payment. There were active collaborators in almost every European country that participated in the Holocaust, the main exception being Denmark where 97 percent of its Jewish population was saved.

The neutral countries were also implicated in the Holocaust. Switzerland guarded its borders zealously and relatively few Jewish refugees found safe haven there during the war. Turkey, under German pressure and because of its own distrust of "minorities," imposed a punitive tax on its Jewish citizens in 1942. This *Varlik Vergisi,* as it was called, impoverished the Jewish community in Turkey. By the time the tax was lifted in the spring of 1944, the Jewish community in Turkey had been brought to its knees, financially and socially. The old canard about "Jewish money controlling the country's economy" and the Jewish "exploiters" had been used to justify this persecution of the Jewish population. After the war, the Turkish Jewish community was only a shell of its former great self and emigration from the country to the West and to the land of Israel picked up pace.

Though most of Sephardic Jewry escaped the ravages of the Holocaust, there were ancient and strong Sephardic communities in the Balkans that were decimated and destroyed. The great Jewish community in the Greek port city of Salonika was shipped en masse to Auschwitz. About 90,000 Greek Jews were killed by the German murder machine. The Jews in Yugoslavia were killed not only by the Germans but by the warring partisan groups as well. The Croatians and Slovenians were particularly cruel to their Jewish neighbors while the Serbs on the whole behaved more fairly and sympathetically to the Jews. The Jews who lived in the Arab countries, in North Africa and in the Middle East, kept a very low profile during the war years. The Arabs were openly pro-German and it was nothing short of miraculous that there were no major killings of Jews in the Arab lands during the war. However, sporadic violence against Jews existed and was accepted in the Arab societies of the Middle East and North Africa throughout the war years.

The Holocaust itself was the culmination of millennia of religious anti-Semitism married to Social Darwinism, crackpot ideology and racial fantasies and backed by an efficient and remorseless killing machine. There is sufficient guilt present in both the Jewish and non-Jewish world regarding inaction during the time of the Holocaust to go around. It is perhaps the saddest chapter ever written in human history, certainly in the modern world that claimed for itself a veneer of civilization and human progress.

The struggle of the Jews to create an independent Jewish state in the land of Israel was fought against the Arabs of Palestine and against the British mandate. By the 1930s, England had repudiated the Balfour Declaration and had no intention of supporting a Jewish national home in Palestine. The Palestinian Arabs conducted a continuing war of terror against the Jewish population and the British, in the main, always sided with the Arabs. Jewish armed resistance fought with the Arabs but also with the British. In 1945, the Labor party swept into office and Ernest Bevin became its foreign minister. Bevin was an avowed anti-Semite and warned the Jews not to "try and push themselves to the head of the queue." England did all in its power to thwart Jewish immigration into Palestine in the immediate aftermath of World War II. It armed the Arabs and attempted to disarm the Jewish militias. Eventually, it tired of the task and left the matter to the United Nations which voted for a partition of the country and the establishment of a Jewish state in Palestine. That state, Israel, came into being in 1948 against the armed objections and invasions of the Arab and Muslim world. The Arab world turned bitterly anti-Jewish with pogroms and expulsions becoming the norm. Eventually most of the Muslim world became *judenrein* with the exception of Morocco and Iran. Arab anti-Semitism imported classical European anti-Semitism to add to its original religious hatreds. All of the conspiracy theories against Jews gained credence in the modern world, and the nineteenth-century anti-Semitic tract, "The Protocols of the Elders of Zion," produced by the Czar's secret police, became widely distributed and believed throughout the Muslim world. This strongly held belief led the Shiite fanatical rulers of Iran at the beginning of the twenty-first century to publicly vow to destroy Israel and its Jews.

The success of the State of Israel, militarily, commercially and socially, attracted worldwide jealousy and enmity. Anti-Semitism now morphed into being anti-Israel. Anti-Israel feeling was legally legitimate and it became the cause of Leftist academia and politicians. Europe once again turned bitterly anti-Semitic under the guise of somehow supporting the Palestinian cause against Israel. The Soviet Union led the anti-Semitic, anti-Israel drive until its collapse in the 1990s. The United Nations became a forum for relentless continuing condemnation of the Jewish state for any pretext whatsoever. Zionism was condemned as being racist and Israel was adjudged by a former president of the United States as being an apartheid nation. Leftist Jews, unfairly blinded by their own alleged liberal values, also joined in the witch hunt against the Jewish state. Continually proposed commercial and academic boycotts, and false war-crimes accusations against Israel for defending itself against Muslim terrorism all created a climate of intense hostility toward Israel, a climate that led to sporadic attacks against Jews in Europe and the United States. Israel could never do anything right; the Palestinians never could do anything considered wrong. Perhaps not all those who were anti-Israel were anti-Semites but certainly all anti-Semites were anti-Israel. So called human rights organizations always took the side of the Palestinians, denying Israel the right to defend itself against indiscriminate murderous terrorism. Herzl had declared that Zionism and the creation of a Jewish state would be the solution for anti-Semitism in human society. Sadly, he was wrong in that assessment. One can even make a convincing case that the existence of the State of Israel has exacerbated the growth of anti-Semitism in world society. This "kosher" anti-Semitism of being anti-Israel has permeated much of the democratic Western world and bodes ill not only for its cowering Jewish populations but as history has shown for the general welfare of those countries themselves. Jews generally and the State of Israel particularly are the canary in the mine. Anti-Semitism eventually destroys the society that nurtures it. Just ask Germany after World War II, the Soviet Union after the 1990 collapse of communism, and the wretched Muslim citizens of the Middle East subject to governmental oppression and societal backwardness. The Talmud tells us that being anti-Jewish is the short-run formula for success, power and popularity but it is also the long-run prescription for decline, if not even disaster. European history is strewn with the self-inflicted wreckage of anti-Semitic states, governments and policies. It is tragic that history continues to repeat itself in this respect.

The pattern of anti-Semitism has been an omnipresent one in Jewish and general history. Though it waxes and wanes in different times and places, it has never completely disappeared. Scholars have told us that it is essentially a non-Jewish problem. That may be theoretically true but it is the Jew that pays the price for its existence. Indoctrination toward tolerance in all educational systems can help alleviate but not completely eliminate this scourge. It is a fact of existence, much like death and taxes, that has to be recognized and somehow dealt with. Simply admitting that it exists can help us deal with the problem. Hard-headed realism instead of fantasy dreams should rule our reaction to anti-Semitism whenever and wherever it raises its ugly head. History's pattern in this instance should be recognizable to all.

Chapter Eleven

Economics, Wealth and Poverty

Judaism does not preach poverty as a noble virtue, though the rabbis of the Talmud note wryly that Judaism and the Jewish nation do somehow deal with poverty better than with wealth. Nevertheless, the rabbis stated that "a poverty-stricken person is considered as though he lives no more." The blessings of the Torah are expressed in physical and materialistic terms – food, wealth, personal independence, security and serenity. In the Mishna and Talmud, the value of work and of earning one's own livelihood without depending upon the largesse of others was extolled. The enormously great Torah scholars, rabbis and teachers of the Talmud and, almost for a millennia thereafter as well, all of the Torah scholars somehow earned their own livelihood. No one was paid for studying or learning Torah or, for that matter, for teaching it to others. Just as the Lord taught Torah to our teacher Moses without compensation, so to speak, so were the Jews to engage in the study of Torah without thought of monetary compensation for so doing. It was only in fourteenth-century Bohemia and Austria, under the brutal conditions of the exile that Jews then suffered, that communities finally began to pay a public salary to rabbis, judges and teachers of Torah. This custom of payment has become the norm in the Jewish world – though there were always exceptions – and continues until today. The communities required and demanded full-time, undistracted spiritual leadership and therefore the rabbis, judges and teachers were paid *sekhar batala* – compensation for the time spent in public service that prevented them from engaging in other professions or trades. This custom of full-time, salaried religious leaders became universal practice amongst the Ashkenazic Jewish world, and to a lesser extent in the Sephardic societies as well. One of the dreams that I have had in my capacity as a rabbi for half a century is to somehow become financially independent and not require a public salary for my time and work. I am certain that almost all rabbis share this very dream but most of us have been unable to realize its fulfillment.

Because of various circumstances that the long exile brought upon the Jewish people and society, it changed from an agriculturally based economy, which it was in Temple times, to one based upon commercial transactions. In the Talmudic period, Jews were engaged in many different occupations, trades and professions including commercial trading, retail sales and importing of silk and flax. Thus, though most Jews earned their bread by manual labor or by being small tradesmen, Jews in the early Middle Ages were already renowned as being excellent traders, bankers (in the Middle Ages this was described more inelegantly as money lenders) and dealers in diamonds and precious stones. Jews in Spain were very active in tax farming, buying the right to collect taxes from the local populace at a discount from the king, or even the mosque or the church, and then collecting the full tax from the hapless citizens. Since the tax collector is always held in local contempt and hatred, this profession only served to further already rampant communal anti-Semitism. Jews were held to be particularly astute in managing the ruler's assets and the national treasury; indeed, Jews served as finance ministers to the rulers of Spain and Portugal during both their Muslim and later Christian periods. Shmuel HaNagid (the prince) and his son Yosef HaNagid, Don Yitzḥak Abrabanel, and Abraham Señor are examples of Jews who rose to manage the finances of kings and their countries. The famed "silk and spice route" from Europe was heavily dominated by Jews and accounted for Jewish communities throughout Asia Minor eventually reaching China. In order to facilitate this route at a time when coinage, burdensome and dangerous to transport long distances, was the only known method of payment, Jews created the rudiments of modern monetary and trade documents – checks, letters of credit, trade bills and other such documents which made the transport of coinage unnecessary. Of course this required a high degree of trust between the parties and thus the commercial organizations of Jews were usually family affairs. As a twelfth-century resident of London noted in his diary: "As long as Simon of York is able to deal with his cousin Solomon of Baghdad and trusts him, there will be salt in London."

But Jews did not easily forsake their love of land and of agricultural pursuits. Many of the famed farms and gardens of Muslim Spain were created and owned by Jews. Jews were in the cattle raising business in Europe for millennia. The famed Rabbi Solomon Yitzḥaki (Rashi) was a well-known and successful vintner in eleventh-century France. His grandson, Rabbi Yaakov ben Me'ir (Rabbeinu Tam), the great scholar and leader of the school of the Tosafists, was a diamond dealer, vintner and money lender. Jews turned to dealing in precious stones since it was a "portable" profession. For centuries, Jews have been most prominent in the diamond trade. Antwerp, New York and Tel Aviv are still major Jewish centers of activity in the diamond industry. Jews became expert cutters, polishers, finishers, and traders in the secretive world of diamond dealing. The Crusades had taught Jews how insecure it was for Jews to live anywhere in Europe. Jews were therefore always on the go and became unable to maintain the temporal stability necessary for agricultural development and expansion. The system of feudalism then present in Europe also militated strongly against Jewish ownership of land and, eventually, many Church and governmental decrees solidified this policy into hard law. Jews oftentimes acted as the managers of the nobleman's estate, being the liaison between the often absent landlord and his impoverished chattels – the peasants and serfs who actually tilled the soil. However, with the thirteenth-century expulsions of the Jews from England and France, the connection of the Jews to any sort of land management in western Europe ended. As Jews migrated eastward in Europe to Germany, Poland, Bohemia and Lithuania, their status as land managers for absentee landlords and noblemen revived. Jews were also active in the liquor trade, manufacturing and selling whiskey and other forms of hard liquor, as well as operating taverns. Even in Talmudic times, the Jews of Babylonia controlled the production and sale of date beer, the drink of choice of that era. As mentioned above, Jews were always active in collecting the rents from the tenant farmers on behalf of the landlords. There were instances again here in the eastern part of Europe of Jews being able to become tax farmers as they had once been in Spain and Portugal. But most eastern European Jews scraped out their minimal existence from manual labor, small farming, logging and small trades such as shoemaking, tailoring, and cooking. Jews were also wagon drivers, porters and grocers. This became the basis of Jewish *shtetl* life in eastern Europe even until the dawn of the twentieth century.

A turning point in the role of Jews in the European economic system occurred in the eighteenth century, mainly through the establishment of rudimentary international banking by the Rothschild family. Freed from the confines of the ghetto, the family was able to branch out from its base in Frankfurt am Main to create banking branches in Paris, London, Vienna and Naples. Soon the Rothschilds became the leading financiers of Europe and amassed a great fortune for themselves on the way. Their success made them folk heroes to the downtrodden and impoverished Jews of Europe, especially those who lay under the heel of the despised Russian Czars. The expression, "As rich as Rothschild" became a Jewish idiom in the *shtetlach* of eastern Europe. This was especially poignant in the eighteenth and nineteenth centuries as the anti-Semitic Czarist decrees drove the vast majority of eastern European Jewry into abject poverty. Locked out from owning land, prevented from attending schools of higher education, limited in participating in many types of trades and possessions, and forced to live within the Pale of Settlement while being arrogatingly taxed, the Jewish economic position was disastrous. The eastern European Jews suffered an unemployment rate as high as forty percent during these times, and an infant mortality rate of close to twenty percent. Malnutrition and illness took a terrible toll on Jews. Their faith and tenacity was sorely tested by these dire physical and economic circumstances. With the rise of urbanization in eastern Europe and its accompanying pressures for secularization, the social and economic infrastructure of the *shtetl* and its traditional way of life began to collapse. It is no wonder that millions of Jews left eastern Europe to search for a better economic life for themselves and their families in far distant shores, mainly the United States, but also Britain, western Europe, South Africa, Canada and South America.

Though the immigrant generations to these new homes faced enormous financial difficulties, the next generation of Jews, the children and grandchildren of the immigrants, rose rapidly both socially and economically. Jews entered the professions – medicine, law, finance, etc. – and were very successful. In the 1840s, Reform German Jews immigrated to the United States and were enormously successful in establishing themselves in investment banking and in major American retailing. The American Civil War provided an opportunity for great wealth, and many Jews profited by it. The later waves of immigration to the United States were not as quickly successful as were the Germans in the 1840s but certainly within a century of their arrival on foreign shores most Jews lived well above the poverty line. The Jewish contribution to sophisticated forms of investment, banking, real estate development, merchandising and commerce generally in modern times is obvious to all. The proficiency of Jews in these areas has always led to a non-Jewish backlash of anti-Semitism. Jews were and are portrayed as economic predators and capitalistic vultures. The anti-Semitic calumny of portraying as Jews as interested only in money and of destroying others because of monetary gain, enshrined in the infamous fabricated anti-Semitic tract "The Protocols of the Elders of Zion," is baked into non-Jewish culture and psyche. From Luther through Marx and later, Jews have been viciously caricatured as being interested only in wealth accumulation and the exploitation of others for their own gain. This canard has taken on a life of its own, and seems so embedded in the non-Jewish world as to defy its justified and necessary eradication.

Paradoxically enough, Jews were also in the forefront of the anticapitalist movements of the nineteenth and twentieth centuries. Marxism in its various offshoots of socialism, communism, Bolshevism, etc. had wide appeal amongst Jews. This was mainly because many of the noble ideals espoused by these ideologies were somewhat akin to Torah values on the subjects of the rights of laborers and employees, social justice, care for the poor, the disadvantaged and the disabled, and a utopian system of fairness and justice for all. Also, the oppression of Czarist Russia against its Jewish population led to the radicalization of much of Jewish youth and their adoption of the red banner. Jews were very active in the trade union movement both in eastern Europe and the United States. The Workmen's Circle/Bund, an all-Jewish labor union, was the largest workers' union in eastern Europe, while the fledgling American Federation of Labor in the United States and the later Amalgamated Clothing Workers as well as the International Ladies Garment Workers Union and the Congress of Industrial Organizations were headed by Jews. Lenin's main allies and cohorts in the Bolshevik takeover of Russia in 1917 were Jews. There was a special powerful and large Jewish "section" in the Soviet Union's Communist Party. It ruthlessly fulfilled its assignment of destroying Jewish religious and national infrastructure in the Soviet Union in the 1920s. Its religion was hatred of religion, especially of its own original faith. It in turn was destroyed by Stalin in his purges and mad campaigns against Jews. Thus ironically, but somewhat truthfully, Jews were castigated from the Right for being communists, and from the Left for being capitalists. This again placed Jews in an absolutely no-win situation, one that was murderously exploited by both Adolf Hitler and by Josef Stalin.

In the field of theoretical economics Jews were very prominent. Many recipients of the Nobel Prize in Economic Sciences in the twentieth century were Jews. In a throwback to medieval times when Jews served as the economic advisers to all of the courts of Europe, Jews were prominent as Ministers of Finance and Secretaries of the Treasury in many countries throughout the world. New ideas as to how to look at economic problems and their solutions, such as game theory, for example, were almost exclusively proposed by Jewish economists and mathematicians. Jews were also capable of great economic frauds, many of which were revealed during the worldwide economic meltdown of 2008. But one should never make the error of confusing Jews with Judaism itself. Individual Jews are always susceptible to all of the vices of the world. This also is a pattern that emerges regularly from Jewish history. Naturally, the individual failings and deceits of the few tarred the many in the eyes of the non-Jewish world. Anti-Semitism based on perceived economic reasons and ingrained national faults is an omnipresent factor in Jewish history. The non-Jewish world is very sensitive with regard to the economic behavior of Jews – much more sensitive that most Jews themselves realize. One Jewish scandal outweighs a dozen Nobel prizes for economics in the public perception of Jews and Judaism. This is also an unfortunately recurring fact of Jewish history.

For many decades the higher echelons of Western world corporations and businesses were *judenrein*. By the end of the twentieth century this situation had changed radically and many a large corporation, insurance company and banking house boasted of principal Jewish roles in managing these mega businesses. All major sports leagues and teams also excluded Jews from ownership and management roles until the latter part of the twentieth century. But as with corporations and financial institutions, Jews became active owners of professional sports teams throughout the Western world. Many of the star professional athletes in all walks of sports life were and are represented by Jewish agents. As is readily understood (or maybe not so readily understood after all) this is a mixed blessing for the Jewish people as a whole. The image of the Jewish sports agent fighting for the last penny (usually it is the last million dollars) confirms the stereotype regarding money and Jews. But Jews feel so comfortable in present-day American society that perhaps many of them do not see any problems. Would that their assessment were correct. However, all of Jewish history speaks against its being so.

The State of Israel, in little more than sixty years of existence, is an economic wonder. It began with a purely socialist government dominated by an all-powerful labor union, the Histadrut. This lethal combination stifled private and foreign investment in the country, created a confiscatory taxation system, established a suffocating governmental bureaucracy and enshrined inefficiency in its banking and monetary policies. However, after thirty years of this the situation slowly changed. Taxes were lowered though they still remained high; the health systems were separated from the Histadrut and made competitive; high-tech industries and companies enticed a significant amount of foreign investment in Israeli companies and innovative Israeli advances in the fields of medicine, science and the arts; and with accompanying exports in all fields of commerce and agriculture, the Israeli economy became vibrant and viable. Israel also benefits from a large hidden economy of donations and support from the world Jewish community to its institutions, religious and educational projects, regional development and welfare agencies. Thousands of Jewish students from foreign lands also stay in Israel for significant periods of time attending its yeshivot, women's seminaries, universities and other schools of higher education. Their contribution to the economy of the country also has significance. Tourism is another significant factor in the Israeli economy. Millions of visitors come to Israel every year and many of them have purchased and maintain homes in Israel and provide other income directly or indirectly to the country's economy. Financial aid to Israel from outside sources, some of them governmental such as American military aid for the purchase of American weapons systems, and in the early decades of the state, reparation payments from Germany, certainly helped Israel get on its feet materially and militarily. Israel has had to integrate into its society millions of immigrants in a short period of time. In spite of all of the inefficiencies, mistakes and failings that were part of this absorption process, Israel's ability to nonetheless do so is nothing short of miraculous. This has to be understood not only on the basis of the country's economy and financial resources, but just as importantly on a basis of social acclimatization. I do not know of any other country that has done so much for so many with so few available resources over such a relatively short period of time.

There are still pockets of poverty in the State of Israel and in the world generally. But the hunger and malnutrition of eastern Europe in the nineteenth and twentieth centuries that plagued its Jewish communities is unknown in Israel. The standard of living is certainly a bit lower in Israel than it is in the United States, but the quality of life is perhaps higher. At least statistics show a higher rate of longevity, satisfaction and optimism in Israel than in almost all of the other developed countries on the globe. Poverty, like wealth itself, is a relative term. The Talmud described true wealth as somehow being satisfied with one's material portion in life. Jews over the ages have suffered great grinding poverty as well as periods of affluence, wealth and material plenty. As King Solomon explains in Proverbs, both wealth and poverty test the spiritual, ethical and behavioral mettle of a person. As mentioned at the beginning of this chapter, on the whole, the patterns of history show that Jews have handled poverty better than wealth, spiritually and religiously speaking. Nevertheless, the Jewish prayer ritual has many specific prayers for material success and bounty. The challenge of money is a major one in life both for those who have a lot of it and for those who feel that they are lacking it. The Talmud teaches us that Moses at Mount Sinai was shown by Heaven a coin made of fire. Fire warms, cooks, lights and sometimes heals. It also burns and destroys, reducing formerly beautiful objects into ashes. This metaphor for money is certainly a descriptively apt one. There is so much good that can be done with money and there is also so much destruction that money, its abundant presence or lack of it, can foment in a home, family or community. Jews have struggled with this dichotomy across the ages. Every family, society and generation struggles anew with this issue. It is one of the basic concerns of living life itself. There is no simple answer that would fit all Jewish individuals, families, and generations. There is no one-size-fits-all solution to this challenge. Blessed are those who are able to successfully navigate these rough waters.

Chapter Twelve

Health and Medicine

Eventually humans come to realize that good health is the greatest blessing that Heaven can bestow upon us. Therefore in the thrice-daily prayer rituals of Judaism, a special prayer for healing and good health is recited. There are particular prayers for restoring good health to the sick that are recited on days of the public reading of the Torah in the synagogue. The Torah itself bids us to guard our health and wellbeing. Human life supersedes almost every other value and commandment in Judaism. Because of this supreme value system of the preservation of life and health at almost all costs, Jews have throughout the ages been skilled practitioners of medicine, pharmacology and health-related fields. In the Bible we find that the great prophets of Israel restored life, health and fertility and were the "physicians" of their time. The Midrash records that our father Abraham was well known as someone who could bring healing to the sick. A medallion around his neck testified to this ability.

The Torah frowned upon quack medicines and magical cures, calling them the "ways of the Amorites," a product of a pagan and superstitious culture. In general the intertwining of health and superstition, always a lethal combination, has been an omnipresent pattern in all of human history and Jewish society was also not immune from its effects. The Talmud refers to a "Book of Healing" that the great Judean king, Hezekiah, removed from circulation. Rashi mentions that he did so because people no longer prayed to God for good health and healing since the remedies to any of their ailments and illnesses could be found in this book. Hezekiah, in order to restore faith and piety amongst his subjects, "buried" the book so it would no longer be available to the sick, forcing them to turn to Heaven for help and succor. Maimonides disagrees vehemently and states that the book was removed because it contained pagan superstitions and quack remedies that in no way could help the patient recover from illness. Maimonides, a famed physician in his time, pointed out that it is unlawful in Judaism to withhold cures from the ill even for imagined spiritual improvement. There still remain vestiges of this dispute between the two views of curing the sick in Jewish life. The mainstream view today is certainly that one should employ the best that modern medicine has to offer for restoring or retaining good health and yet prayer to Heaven is an effective and necessary method of dealing with illness. Neither avenue of help should be ignored or abandoned.

Medicine is an evolving art. The medicine of Talmudic times is not the medicine of the time of Maimonides, nor is the medicine of Maimonides the medicine of the twenty-first century. The later rabbinic scholars of medieval and modern times warned their congregations not to rely upon the medicine, healing methods and cures of the Talmud. "Nature changes" they warned. By this they also meant that the nature of medical knowledge, diagnosis and technology is constantly changing. In our world of x-rays, sonograms, MRIS, CAT scans, extensive and long-running projects of research and experimentation and computerized surgery, one can hardly imagine how medicine was practiced earlier in human history. Much of earlier medicine was therefore pure intuition or guesswork on the part of the doctor. Many times these healers guessed correctly and many times they were not as correct. For instance, bloodletting as a cure for diseases was accepted medical practice well into the twentieth century in Jewish and general society. It was considered an effective method of combating pneumonia and other life-threatening diseases. The Talmud devotes many words and lines to advising the populace regarding proper methods and aftereffects of bloodletting.

The famous barber pole that for centuries adorned the entrance to hair-cutting establishments, had a red stripe in it to denote that blood-letting was also available there. Medicine changes its mind rapidly and sometimes radically. When I was a child growing up in Chicago every Jewish child that I knew had had his or her tonsils removed surgically. In today's world all of my children and grandchildren have, thank God, their marbles and tonsils intact. In Torah knowledge and true spiritual greatness, previous generations are far greater than we are. However, technology generally and medical knowledge particularly has constantly evolved and improved, giving our generation tools for continued health and life that earlier generations did not possess or perhaps even imagine. Judaism has always encouraged the use of the best physicians and medical knowledge available in each generation. One can only judge on the basis of what one then knows and believes. Some of ancient medicine and pharmacology is still valid today. Maimonides long ago preached the health advantages of proper diet, adequate sleep and regular exercise. However, most of medieval medicine – its theories of illnesses and practices of healing – is no longer usable or valuable and should be discarded.

The interest of Jews in medicine is an ongoing pattern in Jewish history. The oldest continuing medical school in Montpelier, Provence, France, was founded by Jewish and Muslim doctors in the eleventh century. Rabbi Moshe ben Naḥman (Ramban) and Rabbi Yehuda HaLevi were famous physicians in medieval Spain. Almost all of the rulers in Europe in medieval and modern times had Jewish doctors on duty at their courts. This was true of the popes of Rome as well. Maimonides writes of his backbreaking schedule as a physician in the court of the Egyptian ruler Saladin, which left him old and fatigued. Nevertheless, the influence of Maimonides on Saladin can be seen in many propitious decrees that Saladin issued in favor of Jewish interests. Stalin had many Jewish doctors take care of him. In his last phase of extreme paranoia and anti-Semitism he hatched the "Doctors Plot" that would not only have killed thirteen Jewish doctors but would have led to a purge and exile of Soviet Jewry generally. He died before his evil intent could be realized. In the United States, official and unofficial *numerus clausus* – maximal quotas inserted in admission policies of medical schools in order to curtail and limit Jewish admissions to those schools – were in force until the 1960s. This is an illustration of the recurring paradox in human civilization of treasuring Jewish contributions to civilization – such as Jewish doctors – while at the same limiting the possibilities of there being any Jewish doctors. A number of Jewish doctors banded together then in postwar America and created medical schools that would allow Jews and other minorities to attend. These included the Chicago Medical School and perhaps most famously the Albert Einstein Medical School affiliated with Yeshiva University. The Jewish community as well as the general American community owes a great debt of gratitude to Dr. Samuel Belkin, the then president of Yeshiva University, for his vision and tenacity in creating the Albert Einstein Medical School. These institutions teach the art of healing, and healing is doing God's work here on earth. One of the great advantages of American medical schools today is that they have created and maintain programs and fellowships that allow observant Jews to attend and graduate from these institutions and become physicians. Nowadays, the observant Jewish doctor is a fixture in clinics, medical offices and hospitals throughout the Western world. This is also a most positive development in the evolution of proper medical practice in civilization.

Over the past half century it has become clearly obvious that smoking tobacco is injurious to one's health and longevity. Yet in many parts of the Jewish world smoking is considered traditional. In general society, teenage smoking is considered "cool" and a very immature sign of maturity. For some, this habit is considered to be a vestige of the good old days of eastern European society when smoking amongst yeshiva students was endemic and Hasidic masters were inveterate pipe smokers. Tobacco was considered medicinal when it was first introduced in Europe in the late seventeenth and early eighteenth century. As late as the early twentieth century, tobacco companies advertised their lethal products as being good for one's health and well-being and especially beneficial in aiding proper digestion of food. Permission to smoke tobacco products on Jewish Holidays was rabbinically granted on the premise that tobacco fell under the rubric of "*okhel nefesh*" – that it was essentially a food product and thus could be "cooked" or burned on Holidays. In the Sephardic world where smoking often involved the use of a *nargila* (water pipe, or hookah), smoking on the Holidays was associated with drinking, which was the basis of the leniency that allowed it in that society. Naturally, modern medical knowledge has uprooted these premises so that there is no longer any true physical basis for this leniency. However, since smoking is addictive, today even the pious smokers still smoke on the Holidays.

Smoking was also originally seen as a spiritual experience. Kabbalists and Hasidic masters saw holy visions in the swirling smoke of cigarettes, cigars and pipes. We have records of great men of the Sephardic world who used hashish or other kinds of hallucinogenic substances in their water pipes. They claimed that they were then able to see visions of heaven and thus intensify their prayer service. Of course in modern parlance we would say that they were unfortunately stoned. In the yeshiva world of nineteenth- and twentieth-century eastern Europe, the land of Israel and the United States, almost everyone – the faculty and the students – smoked tobacco. When the harmful health factors of tobacco were finally discovered and popularized in the second half of the twentieth century, smoking was drastically curtailed in the American yeshivot but only moderately so in the Israeli institutions. Rabbinic bans against smoking were issued, but those who were already addicted to it found it hard to stop smoking and their presence in the educational institutions and in society generally encouraged the younger students to begin smoking. Thus a vicious circle of harmful health habits was and is perpetuated. Social pressures, the desire for the young to feel independent and mature, and the addictive nature of nicotine in tobacco products all conspire to defeat the best efforts of educators and doctors to remove tobacco completely from the Jewish scene. But the effort to do so should be continued and intensified. In most cases it is a long-term prescription for health suicide. Thus, within a century, tobacco use switched from being a healthy and spiritually enhancing experience to becoming a dreaded health hazard. The constant in Jewish life is to obey all currently proven and accepted medical advice as to maintaining good health and prolonging life. It is the pattern of medical knowledge that changes – not the positive Jewish attitude toward health and life-giving cures and methods.

Alcoholism was practically unknown in the Jewish world until our times. The Jews of eastern Europe were heavily engaged in the liquor business, but they did not overly imbibe themselves. They drank but hardly ever to drunkenness. The popular Yiddish ballad sung in Jewish homes in eastern Europe contrasted the drunkenness of their non-Jewish neighbors with their own sober, spiritual and prayerful behavior. Only on Purim and on Simḥat Torah was drunkenness socially acceptable and that was also within the confines of the home, study hall or synagogue. Street drunkenness was abhorred in Jewish society as was frequenting a tavern or a bar. However, as Jews became assimilated and secularized both in Israel and in the United States, drinking became socially acceptable and the Jewish rate of alcoholism rose dramatically, equaling that of the general population. All of the diseases endemically associated with alcoholism now invaded Jewish society as well. It especially became acceptable for young people to drink liquor at bar and bat mitzva or Shabbat parties, starting those young people down a very slippery slope of association with alcohol. Synagogues in the United States aware of this problem began to ban the serving of hard liquor on their premises, even at catered affairs such as weddings and banquets. Wine was always consumed in the Jewish home but mainly in conjunction with the fulfillment of ritual obligations. As table wine became more popular in Jewish society in the latter part of the twentieth century, the necessity for restraint, discipline and moderation in matters of alcoholic beverages increased. Modern Jewish society has a problem with alcohol. Wild drinking on Purim has cost lives. The true consequences of drinking alcohol have yet to make the desired impression on modern Jewish society. It is a serious health issue.

Eastern European Jews were also addicted to snuff tobacco. The snuff container was passed around the synagogue regularly and the prayer services were often accompanied by loud sneezing. This habit was socially accepted in eastern European society. However, the children of the immigrant generation in America, and in Israel as well, found it to be unappealing and it has almost disappeared completely from Jewish society today. Though the use of snuff tobacco was widespread in the seventeenth and eighteenth century, its waning popularity in general society is reflected in its dramatic decline in Jewish society as well. Unfortunately the use of marijuana, heroin and other powerfully addictive drugs is rampant in societies the world over today. Jewish society, even the religious observant sector, has not been immune to this scourge. All campaigns against the use of drugs amongst the young have unfortunately been inadequate, and ignoring or denying its presence in our society is certainly not the way to deal with this enormous problem. As yet, there has not been a coordinated, cooperative attitude and program to combat the appearance of drugs in our schools. Many schools simply want to sweep the matter under the rug and not admit that their august institution could have such a problem. This type of attitude and behavior does a disservice to all concerned – the school, the student and the community.

Jewish society, and Ashkenazic Jewry particularly, suffers from certain types of genetically caused diseases. This is a result of close inbreeding within the same, relatively small ethnic group over many centuries. It was also common in eastern European society for first cousins to marry each other. These factors induced an incidence of dreaded genetic disorders and diseases amongst Jewish children such as Tay-Sachs and Gaucher's disease among others. Advances in genetic testing and understanding of the cause of these diseases led to a program that tested Jewish young men and women for the possibility of their being a carrier of one of these diseases. Each young person was assigned a number and before courting one another the numbers were compared to see if both of them contained this genetic disease carrier. This program, created and promoted by a family that had itself lost children to Tay-Sachs, has in effect over the past twenty years dramatically cut the rate of the incidence of these diseases amongst the Jewish community. Nevertheless, for various personal and emotional reasons there are those who are determined to beat the genetic odds and therefore these diseases have not as yet been completely eliminated.

It has also been noted by research and medical studies that Jews are more susceptible to certain chronic diseases than the average person in the general population. Diabetes is one of those diseases. The increase in obesity in the Western world generally has had a concurrent effect in Jewish society as well. The traditional eastern European Jewish diet, laden with salt, fat and meat is certainly no longer regarded as being a healthy one. Yet it persists in most Ashkenazic Jewish homes, especially on Shabbat and Holidays. Whether health reasons alone can overcome the traditions and ingrained taste buds of the Ashkenazic community remains to be seen. Over the centuries there simply did not exist many fruits and vegetables in eastern Europe and thus a taste for cauliflower, broccoli, zucchini, citrus fruits, etc., never could flourish. We all develop a liking for the menu that we are accustomed to. We are all creatures of habit and therefore radical changes in our food diet are very hard to accomplish. But there is no doubt that the eating habits and foods of the current Jewish society are changing and hopefully this will lead to better health and longer life.

In matters of mental health there has also been a great change in Jewish society. The attitude toward using mental-health experts as part of our lives has today become acceptable in most sections of Jewish society. The social shame of visiting a therapist or a psychologist or a psychiatrist has slowly abated. The presence of many observant Jews in the field of mental health has broken down many previously sacrosanct social barriers in Jewish society regarding getting help in matters of mental and emotional health. Depression, addiction, narcissism, dementia and other forms of mental and emotional problems abound in general society and are strongly present in Jewish society as well. Marriage counseling – even divorce counseling – are today accepted as necessary tools in Jewish family life.

The development of modern medicine's ability to provide children to previously infertile couples has also had a profound effect on the emotional well-being of the family. Other medical advances such as contraception and the treatment of physical intimacy problems, have required halakhic input and rabbinic decisors have taken on the task of guiding observant Jews in these matters. The halakha has risen to deal with all of these issues decisively yet discreetly.

As modern medicine continues to discover more knowledge about our bodies, minds and emotions, Jewish law and rabbinic studies are keeping apace with these advances. What we think we know medically today, may be disproved tomorrow by deeper and more thorough studies. But we can only function on the basis of our current accepted knowledge and practice. The Talmudic maxim teaches, "A judge can decide only upon what his eyes currently see." Again, Judaism stands for life and for quality of life and any medical advances that promote these goals are gladly incorporated into Jewish life and law. We believe that Heaven helps those that help themselves first. The Torah's admonition to "guard carefully your self [health] and your life" (Deuteronomy 4:9) is the guiding rule regarding all matters of health and medicine. It is a supreme value in Judaism.

Chapter Thirteen

Rabbis, Teachers and the Lay Community

I have previously written another book on the subject of rabbis and the lay community. Entitled *Tending the Vineyard,* it details the challenges and vicissitudes of the modern-day rabbi in the Western world and particularly in the United States. One of the salient points made in that book is that the role of the rabbi in Jewish life is constantly changing and evolving depending upon times, circumstances and locations. And though the role of the rabbi in Jewish life dates back to our teacher and leader Moses, there have been many changes and adaptations to that role over the long millennia of Jewish history. There is one constant, however, that marks all ages and locations. And that is the constant degree of tension that exists – in fact that must exist – between the rabbi and his community. The Talmud taught us that a rabbi that is extremely popular and has no opposition or critics present in his community is obviously not fulfilling his rabbinic role properly. To which Rabbi Yisrael Lipkin of Salant, the great nineteenth-century founder of the *Musar* (ethical behavior) movement, added that a rabbi who is universally disliked by his community is also a failed rabbi and human being. And so the rabbi has always been a tightrope walker, attempting to balance the true spiritual goals and needs of the community with his own personal community status and approbation. The tension thus created has marked Jewish communal life throughout the ages.

We find that in biblical times the prophets of Israel were subject to communal and governmental abuse, physically and verbally. People do not like to be chastised and have their faults dwelt upon by religious authority. Isaiah had his beard pulled from his cheeks; Jeremiah sat in a dungeon as a prisoner; the great Elijah was persecuted unmercifully, and the list continues. Yet there were prophets who enjoyed public approbation and great influence such as Samuel, Gad and Nathan. The prophets of the early Second Commonwealth such as Zechariah, Haggai and Malachi were also of great influence and highly respected. Ezra and Nehemiah worked a revolution in Jewish life in the founding of the Second Commonwealth against determined opposition. Ezra punished those Jews who would not return to the land of Israel and, in turn, legend has it that he was cursed by his opponents not to be buried in the Holy Land. This legend is the origin of "Ezra's Tomb," located today in southern Iraq. In any event, throughout the Second Temple period the rabbis of Israel were constantly engaged in struggle against their physical and religious enemies, the Hellenist Jews, the Sadducees, the Essenes, the Herodian rulers of the country, the early Christians and the Roman sympathizers among the Jews. All of these struggles are recorded for us in the Mishna, the Talmud, Josephus and other sources. The rabbis then were a political as well as a spiritual force in the Jewish community. In the emerging Diaspora of the time in Rome and Babylonia, Egypt and Cyrenaica, the rabbis assumed spiritual and sometimes temporal leadership of those communities. Most of their efforts were dedicated to strengthening Jewish education for the masses and combating the pagan influences of Roman and Greek culture that were then dominant. Great academies of Torah learning were formed in the land of Israel as well as in Babylonia and the decisions emanating from those academies were followed throughout the Jewish world. None of the rabbis of the time received a salary for their communal efforts or teaching, all of them being employed in various types of work and commerce. At that time, serving as a rabbi or teacher was a purely voluntary non-remunerative role.

Nevertheless, the Talmud records for us the tensions and disagreements that often surfaced between the rabbis and the heads of the Torah academies and the general Jewish communities where they resided. Almost all of the great academies of Torah learning located in Nehardea, Sura, Pumbadita, Mata Meḥasya, Pum Nahara, Meḥoza and Neresh experienced open hostility from the local Jewish populations. In addition, the presence of a temporal leader of Babylonian Jewry, the *Reish Galuta*/Exilarch, often caused great friction between the rabbis of the Torah academies and local communities, and the *Reish Galuta* himself. The Talmud records for us extreme cases where the local rabbi or head of the academy was arrested by the *Reish Galuta,* imprisoned and even executed! The line of demarcation between the authority of the *Reish Galuta* on one side, and the rabbis and the heads of the Torah academies on the other, was apparently simple and clear – the rabbis were in charge of spiritual matters and the *Reish Galuta* was in charge of all temporal matters of the community. But there were many instances when there was no agreement between them as to which issues were to be considered spiritual and which temporal. This fault line runs throughout Jewish history regarding the relationship of the rabbi to the lay leadership of the community. The Talmud boldly stated that the rabbi is responsible for all communal matters. The lay leadership of Jewish communities has mainly dissented from that opinion. A sad example of this was the decades-long dispute between Rabbeinu Sa'adia Gaon and the *Reish Galuta* in ninth-century Babylonia that led to the ouster of Sa'adia Gaon as head of the Torah academy at Sura.

As mentioned earlier, rabbis received no salary for their communal work until fourteenth-century Austria and Bohemia. The pressures of the exile and the necessities of the community required full-time rabbinic attention. This unavoidable change in the relationship of the rabbi to the lay community would serve to decrease the rabbi's independence while enhancing the control of the lay leaders over him. Furthermore, the salary of the rabbi, usually either too little from the rabbi's point of view, too much from the point of view of the community, or both, always remained a point of contention and constant negotiation between the parties. As can now easily be seen, the tension between the rabbi and the community was essentially built into the system. There were many communities that rose above such tensions in a harmonious and wise fashion. But there were very many other communities that were torn apart by the divisions created by such a system of tension and argument over turf and wages. Many times the disputes over the rabbi led to non-Jewish governmental intervention as for example the bitterly fought cases in eighteenth-century Altona/Hamburg and in Vilna. The Altona/Hamburg controversy centered around the personality and spiritual writings of Rabbi Yehonatan Eybeschütz. The Vilna controversy over Rabbi Shmuel Avigdor led to the lay leaders of that community placing a rock on his rabbinic chair and not allowing anyone to become rabbi of the community! A rabbi in Vilna did not arise again until the 1920s when the Polish government, then ruling Vilna, insisted that the Jewish community hold elections to choose a communal rabbi. These apparently local controversies affected other communities and became worldwide in scope and influence, thereby serving to undermine the position and authority of the rabbis in many other European communities of the time.

Inter-rabbinic disputes also weakened the authority of the rabbis in the eighteenth and nineteenth centuries in Europe. Famous disputes, as for instance over a divorce decree granted in Kleve and contested by the parties with rabbinic support on both sides of the issue, or the controversy between Rabbi Yaakov Emden and Rabbi Yehonatan Eybeschütz over the granting of kabbalistic amulets that allegedly were associated with the apostate false messiah Shabbetai Tzvi, rocked the rabbinic world. The *eiruv*, a halakhic "fence" that encloses a community and allows Jews to carry on Shabbat, was instituted by King Solomon in biblical times to promote harmony, peace and Shabbat social life. However, over the ages and in our times as well, it has been a constant source of inter-rabbinic dispute to the extent that many a community has been bitterly divided over an *eiruv* approved by some rabbinic authorities and disapproved by other rabbis. Almost all major Jewish communities had an *eiruv* throughout Jewish history and most Jewish communities today also have an *eiruv*. Unfortunately, almost invariably with the benefits of the *eiruv* comes rabbinic dispute and divided communities. This apparently is an unavoidable, continually recurring pattern in Jewish life. It is undoubtedly not what King Solomon had in mind. Matters of *kashrut* supervision, especially in twentieth-century America and Israel also gave rise to bitter inter-rabbinic wrangling and public dispute. And when *kashrut* supervision both in Israel and in America evolved into large "businesses" then the disputes and disparagements on all sides intensified. Rabbis, like Jews generally, are sometimes contentious individuals.

The rise of the Hasidic movement also undermined rabbinic authority in eastern and central Europe in the nineteenth and twentieth centuries. The Hasidic rebbe became the authority for his followers in all matters, halakhic, spiritual and mundane. The rebbe, unlike the communal rabbi, had no communal governing board to answer to, though he was subject to his popularity rating amongst the masses. In addition, the nineteenth century saw the rise of urbanization, Enlightenment, secularization, mass emigration and radicalism amongst eastern European Jews, especially the younger generation. The rabbi of the community was often the victim of these trends which he was unable to combat successfully. Great rabbis such as Rabbi Me'ir Leibush Malbim were driven from their rabbinic posts by community governing bodies that were now representative of these disturbing anti-traditional trends and ideologies. Further complicating the situation and weakening the authority of the communal rabbi was the rise of the yeshiva movement, especially in Lithuania and Slovakia in the nineteenth century. The *rosh yeshiva* – the head of the yeshiva – was an alternate figure of Torah authority to the communal rabbi. In order to combat this problem at first, the head of the yeshiva served simultaneously as the rabbi of the community as well. However, with the rise of newer and more numerous yeshivot this arrangement could no longer be universal.

The traditional eastern European rabbi was mainly a scholar, an author of Torah works. He was not what in today's world would be called a pastoral rabbi. Many times he had with him in the community a colleague who served as a *dayan* – a judge and halakhic decisor – to whom all questions of Jewish law and monetary disputes were referred, and the rabbi continued with his scholarship without distraction. The typical rabbi only spoke publicly and at length twice a year on the Shabbat preceding Yom Kippur and the one preceding Pesaḥ. There were *maggidim* – usually itinerant preachers – who visited the communities regularly and held public addresses and lectures. Larger communities such as Vilna had permanent *maggidim* function in their societies. Thus, because of all of the factors discussed above, the communal rabbi's role in eastern European society was severely diminished by the time the twentieth century began. Since many of the smaller communities were perennially impoverished and the community's public budget was in a constant state of debt, this situation was exploited by wealthy Jews to "purchase" the post of rabbi for a relative of theirs and this also contributed to a weakened authority of the rabbi so installed. In effect the system became corrupted. And it became further corrupted by the rise of differing political parties within Jewish society in the late nineteenth century. The newly elected rabbi was often beholden to the political party that had backed his candidacy and was thus acutely handicapped in his communal authority and influence, especially over members of the other political parties that had not backed him. The communal rabbi of pre–World War II eastern Europe was thereby compromised by factors not of his choosing, nor were they really subject to his control. It is no wonder, therefore, that the typical yeshiva student of this time disdained the rabbinate if not even rabbis themselves; a trend, by the way, that continues till today. It truly was not the profession or vocation for a good, smart Jewish boy.

The situation of rabbis outside of eastern Europe was varied and volatile. In the 1800s English Jewry adopted a system of installing a chief rabbi to head the Orthodox organization, the United Synagogue. The first chief rabbi was Rabbi Nathan Adler of Germany who was recommended for the post (over the other prominent candidate Rabbi Samson Raphael Hirsch) by Queen Victoria herself. The increasing numbers of eastern European immigrants, as well as the arrival of Hasidim in England, chipped away at the hegemony of the United Synagogue and its chief rabbi. However the institution of the Chief Rabbi in England still functions today and rather well at that. This is undoubtedly a testament to the caliber of the leaders and scholars who have filled this role over almost two centuries. The Chief Rabbi system also operates in South Africa, and there, too, it has remained vital and influential. In France the Consistoire of Paris established the post of *Grand Rabbin* which still exists today. Chief rabbis also appeared sporadically within some of the pre–World War I Jewish communities of the Austro-Hungarian Empire. All of this was further complicated by the rise of Reform and

Liberal groupings that contested and many times overcame the Orthodox hegemony over the post of Chief Rabbi. Thus there was created a subtle but strong objection to the entire chief rabbinate system. In the ensuing paragraphs we will see how this affected the attitude of many in the land of Israel to the institution of such a system there. In the United States the attempt to establish a system of chief rabbis failed to take hold. An attempt to appoint a chief rabbi in New York (the appointee was Rabbi Yaakov Yosef of Vilna) failed, ending in bitter disputes and heartbreak. The same was true of the fate of Rabbi Yaakov David Wilovsky (Ridvaz) who was appointed Chief Rabbi of Chicago at the beginning of the twentieth century and was driven from town by unscrupulous meat purveyors. However, St. Louis was able to establish a successful Chief Rabbi system that lasted till the twenty-first century. In general, American Jewry was too rootless, diverse and chaotic for any coherent system of a rabbinate to be established. So it was that every American rabbi found himself basically on his own in whatever congregation or community he found employment. This factor had a profound influence in changing the very nature and job description of the American rabbi in the twentieth century.

In the early 1920s under the British mandate in then Palestine, the Jewish *yishuv* established a Chief Rabbi system with Rabbi Avraham Yitzḥak HaKohen Kook serving as the first Ashkenazic Chief Rabbi and as the driving force behind the entire project. A Sephardic Chief Rabbi, the *Rishon LeTziyon,* was also chosen to serve in tandem with his Ashkenazic counterpart. Sephardic and Ashkenazic chief rabbis were likewise appointed for the main Jewish cities of the country. However, there was opposition to this system, especially amongst the anti-Zionist members of the *yishuv hayashan* (the original Jewish settlers of Jerusalem in the 1800s.) This group set up in effect an alternate rabbinic system headed then by Rabbi Yosef Ḥayyim Sonnenfeld, and called itself the Eda HaḤaredit. It also operated an independent *kashrut* supervision system in competition with that of the official Chief Rabbi. This situation continued even after the establishment of the State of Israel. By the 1980s, the official Israeli rabbinate declined in influence and was viewed by many as merely a governmental bureaucracy, paid and supported by a government budget and subject to much political horse trading, which basically governed matters of marriage and divorce, religious infrastructure and ritual law but was somehow disconnected from the everyday life of the citizens of Israel. Attempts have been made to create a more independent, apolitical, communal-type rabbinate in Israel but this type of rabbi is still a rarity in Israeli society. Nevertheless, there are now far more communal and synagogue-centered rabbis operating in Israel, most of them being outside the official umbrella of the Chief Rabbinate and the Ministry of Religions which is currently operated by the Prime Minister's office.

Part of the opposition in religious circles to the Israeli Chief Rabbi system is based in the memory bank of the Jewish people. In the 1800s in Russia, under pressure from the Jewish "enlightened ones" who opposed Jewish tradition, the Russian government, anti-Semitic to the core, instituted an official rabbinate system in Russia. These rabbis were called in Jewish society, "*rav mita'am*," a somewhat derogatory term meaning that they were government-appointed rabbis with no real rabbinic standing in terms of religious authority and scholarship. Some of these rabbis, such as Rabbi Yaakov Mazeh of Moscow, performed ably on behalf of the Jewish people vis-à-vis the Czarist authorities. Many, however, were complete charlatans if not even traitors to their people. This experience of eastern European Jewry with an official, government-sanctioned rabbinate left a bad taste in the mouths of their descendants toward any system of a chief rabbinate, especially one that was again instituted by governmental authority, even Jewish governmental authority. Indeed, the establishment of a rabbinic seminary publicly dedicated to the goal of producing not only theoretical Torah scholars but practicing rabbis, was looked at askance in the yeshiva world. The Sephardic world also had a chief rabbinate system under the Ottoman Empire – the *Ḥakham Bashi* – but again it was more a symbolic position than one of great influence or leadership. That was reserved for the recognized scholars and holy men of the Sephardic world. Rav Kook's dream of a chief rabbinate in the land of Israel that would provide moral and spiritual guidance above political pandering and factionalism, and which would be of influence and counterbalance to a secular ruling government in the country, unfortunately was never fully realized. It still awaits its redemption and revitalization today.

In the United States in the first half of the twentieth century, the traditional American rabbinate was still dominated by rabbis born and trained in Europe. Because of the harsh monetary conditions of the then American rabbinate, many of these rabbis were engaged in private *kashrut* supervision. However, as the Conservative movement was gaining in strength and popularity and its seminary was producing American-born and American-trained rabbis, the Orthodox yeshivot were forced to produce their own homegrown rabbis. The Rabbi Isaac Elchanan Theological Seminary (which grew into Yeshiva University), Hebrew Theological College in Chicago, Ner Israel Rabbinical Seminary in Baltimore, and many New York based yeshivot such as Mesivta Torah VoDaas and Yeshivat Rabbeinu Chaim Berlin also began to graduate American-born rabbis and situate them in communities. These rabbis were English speaking and pastoral in their outlook and conduct of their rabbinical positions. Gradually the Orthodox American rabbinate became a much more user-friendly institution, not so much based solely upon pure scholarship, though scholarship was certainly still emphasized, as on personal contact and family and communal guidance. Strong rabbinical personalities helped build the Day School movement, the key factor in the revitalization of Jewish life in America. Rabbinic leadership was at the forefront of many important accomplishments – support for the State of Israel, removal of bias and discrimination against Jews and other minorities in American commercial and educational institutions, the plight of Russian Jewry, etc. – and this helped boost the leadership status of the local rabbis in all of their community endeavors. Great rabbinic decisors such as Rabbi Moshe Feinstein appeared on the American scene and, in a sense, their presence freed the local rabbis from having to deal solely with complex halakhic issues, allowing them to concentrate their efforts on their communities and congregations. The weekly sermon, teaching classes, writing bulletins and messages, visiting the sick, attending and officiating at life-cycle events, all became the regular fare of the American synagogue rabbi. Rabbinic salaries, mainly outside of the New York area, became much more commensurate with the true costs of living and of the entertaining and hospitality expected of the rabbi and his family. However, the tension between the rabbi and the lay leadership of congregations is a constant pattern in Jewish life everywhere. Since, in the course of human events, no congregation is completely satisfied with its rabbi and no rabbi is completely satisfied with his congregation, this pattern remains an abiding one.

The development of smaller insular congregations and the demise of many "cathedral" synagogues in the current Jewish world have also been a cause of diminished rabbinic influence. Many if not most of these smaller congregations do not have a rabbinic leader per se, and would not be economically viable if they had to shoulder the responsibility of paying a full-time rabbinic salary. The "Shabbat rabbi" has become a recognized institution in much of the American Jewish scene and here in Israel as well. It takes almost superhuman effort to be a successful "Shabbat rabbi." Usually both the rabbi and the congregation are mutually dissatisfied with the arrangement but it survives because of financial and organizational necessity. Many graduates of yeshivot continue to pray in the yeshiva long after leaving the yeshiva itself. Their spiritual mentor and guide usually remains the head of the yeshiva, who often does not see himself as being able or obligated to fulfill the role of the community or synagogue rabbi. There are major exceptions to this assessment and there are certain communities where the heads of the yeshivot are the main activists in that community. But this is certainly more the exception than the general rule. Thus the position of rabbi is still evolving in the United States and Israel today. What was successful in the nineteenth or twentieth century in the European or Ottoman rabbinate may no longer be even relevant in twenty-first-century Jewish society.

There was a time in Jewish history when the rabbinate attracted the best and the brightest and most talented of Jewish youth. With the opening of vast opportunities in other professions to Jewish young men today in the Diaspora and Israel, there are not that many superior candidates for the rabbinate any longer. The scholars yearn to head yeshivot of their own, and are instantly and many times inadvertently transformed into full-time fundraisers. A more educated laity, products of yeshiva education themselves, has been a mixed blessing to today's rabbi. His authority is more greatly challenged by a laity that feels itself to be the rabbi's equal in scholarship and rabbinic decision making, but such a laity can also provide a much more fertile field in which a rabbi might institute Torah-strengthening programs and foster communal achievements. Certainly efforts should be made in the yeshivot to encourage promising young scholars to enter the rabbinate and to provide them with the skills of communication that are so necessary in today's world to be an effective leader. This will require a change in the mindset of many of the heads of today's yeshivot that retain the almost traditional yeshiva disdain for the rabbinate and rabbis. It will also require a greater effort by the laity of Jewish communities to attract properly trained and talented rabbis to their synagogues and communities. Perhaps there is no one rabbi that is truly indispensable for the success of a particular Jewish community or synagogue. But the institution of the rabbinate in all of its differing evolving forms over the long centuries of Jewish life appears to be indispensable to Jewish life and growth.

Chapter Fourteen

Legends, Fantasies and Falsifications

Legends are necessary for nation building and community cohesiveness. Legends about heroic people and events are not necessarily accurate, though they certainly serve the purpose of somehow characterizing and defining the persona and/or the event. Legends of holy and pious people and legends about villains and the wicked are often subject to fabrication and gross exaggeration, but the legend leaves no doubt in the minds of later generations as to who was the holy and pious person and who was the villain. Judaism deals with legends in a wholesale fashion. Midrash is probably the main conveyor of legend to Jews as far as the biblical and Talmudic periods are concerned. However, there is a plethora of legends about great Jews throughout the centuries that exists in an oral and sometimes also written fashion. Hasidism abounds with legend and stories regarding its rebbes and other assorted holy men. The great rebbe of Kotzk, Rabbi Menaḥem Mendel Morgenstern (Halperin) said the definitive word about all of these legends and stories: "He who believes all of these tales is a fool and yet he who states that they could not have occurred is a non-believer (*apikores*)." Many times there are legends that contradict one another. This should not faze us, for again, each legend comes to emphasize a particular insight into an event or a personality trait of a great person and does not declare the statement it makes as fact. Midrash is full of contradictory statements and opinions about the very same incident or person but this in no way compromises the value of Midrash to us as a conduit of Jewish values and insights. It is only when Midrash and legends are taught as facts that these problems of contradictions and obvious exaggerations arise.

The Jewish people as a whole possess a strong collective memory. We remember leaving Egypt on a Thursday and standing at Mount Sinai and receiving the Torah on Shabbat. We remember all of the glories of Solomon's Temple in Jerusalem as we do the Babylonian exile and the story of Purim. Ezra and the Second Temple, the Hasmoneans and Herod as well are all stored in our genetic memory cells. The events of the long exile and of our longing to return home to Zion and Jerusalem are a significant part of our memory bank. This memory bank has been fed by stories about great people, significant events and terrible tragedies that have occurred over the millennia of Jewish life. These legends, whether completely accurate or not, help us recall the core event and/or person about which they revolve and, in so doing, keep our memory of the past alive enabling us to deal so much better with our present situations and challenges. A people cannot survive for long having lost its memory. Most of the secular Jewish world today suffers from this type of amnesia regarding its past. There was a Jewish people before 1897 and the Zionist movement, before the Holocaust and before 1948 and the establishment of the State of Israel. Ignoring and ridiculing Jewish legend, even when one is seemingly historically or empirically correct in so doing, helps destroy accurate Jewish memory as well. One must be careful to remove and differentiate legend from fact. But legend should nevertheless be retained for it casts light and shadow, nuance and insight on the facts that we do know and have at hand. Facts are knowledge while legend oftentimes is pure inspiration. It is legend and Midrash that create sermons, dreams, goals and action in the Jewish world. It is legend that has contributed to the revival of Jewish life in individuals and communities over the past decades. Legend is to be treasured.

Nevertheless, as mentioned above, the main problem with legend is that it is often translated into reality and fact and replaces the simple understanding of words and events that appear in the Torah. The Talmud was well aware of this tendency and therefore stated: "A verse in the Torah never loses its plain simple meaning." Rabbi Shmuel ben Me'ir (Rashbam), the grandson of Rabbi Shlomo Yitzḥaki (Rashi) in eleventh-century France, chided his grandfather for wandering too far away from this principle in Rashi's immortal commentary to Torah. Rashi agreed with the thrust of his grandson's words but even so, never revised his commentary. Rabbi Abraham ibn Ezra struggled mightily to separate legend from fact in his Torah commentary. So did Don Yitzḥak Abrabanel and Rabbi Ovadya Sforno. Even in the Talmud there is strong criticism of "those who continually distort the plain meaning of the verse" and substitute legend for it. But as any pulpit rabbi having to deliver a sermon every Shabbat to his long-suffering congregation will tell you, it is the stuff of legend that piques the interest of an audience and captivates it. The Talmud/Midrash records for us that Rabbi Akiva, while delivering a public Torah lecture, saw that his audience was dozing off and therefore switched immediately from his prepared subject text and introduced Midrash and legend into his speech to rekindle the audience's interest and regain its attention. So, the quest for the perfect balance in this matter still continues in the pulpit, the classroom and in the works of commentary to Torah and Judaism. The Talmud has been eminently successful in achieving such a balance when discussing the past of Israel and its biblical heroes and leaders. It records everything, hides nothing and yet preserves legend as the essential understanding of the person and the situation.

Legend is also the stuff of much of Jewish biography of its great people. There is an admonition in Judaism not to speak ill of the dead. There are also halakhic restraints on what can be said about the living as well. Slander has a very broad definition in Judaism and thus even the "truth" is oftentimes prohibited from being said or printed in many circumstances. All of this naturally creates somewhat of a vacuum regarding the true events and behavior patterns of the lives of famous people and then, inexorably, legend rushes in to fill that vacuum. Thus most Jewish biography in the religious world of Judaism is fanciful, hagiographic and laden with anecdotes and stories, some of which are too fantastic and incredible for even to the most naïve to believe. Sometimes the real person being described is lost in the welter of legend and stories served up in such biographies. Yet it is clear that the very existence of a legend can tell us something about the person. Two men once exchanged stories about a great sage for whom fantastic claims of spirituality and piety were being made. One asked, "Do you really believe that story?" The other replied, "No, I do not. But no one tells such stories about the two of us."

Thus legend does in fact tend to be valuable in assessing the character and achievements of great figures of the Jewish past and present. Again, the caveat in all of this remains the ability to remember that it is legend and not necessarily reality that one is dealing with in such matters. And the Jewish penchant for legend is so strong that when books of true biography, warts and all, are written about great Jewish figures, these works usually face withering criticism if not even outright bans from religious circles. This is not only true in the Jewish world. Generally speaking, all peoples prefer legend over reality. American schoolchildren and their parents and teachers wish to believe that George Washington never told a lie and that he threw a coin across the Potomac River. In the realm of nation building and national unity, discarding legend can prove to be very damaging to the development of national pride and civil unity. It is ironic that dictatorial and totalitarian regimes have always successfully exploited legend to further its aims to a far greater extent than have more benign regimes and governments. Legend is a most powerful tool. Like all powerful tools it is also terribly dangerous when misused.

Many times legend becomes myth. Myth is a sense of human recognition that the story being told is not factual but it nevertheless changes legend from history or biography into literature and philosophy – sometimes sacred holy literature and philosophy. For instance, there is an opinion in the Talmud that Job as a person never existed, and that the entire book of Job is an allegory introduced into the holy canon of the Bible to teach us the philosophy and worldview of Judaism on the subjects of reward and punishment, man's travails on earth and the inscrutability of the divine will as reflected in our lives. Myth is therefore much more philosophical than mere legend. It transcends this "real" world to discuss and teach values and insights that are eternal and almost never changing in the human existence. It provides the background lighting for our brief appearance on the stage of life. The *Musar* movement as well as Hasidic teachings, when analyzing the legends of Midrash and the Talmud, elevated many of these legends into a mythological view of Judaism and human behavior. Legend teaches us how to view others and events; myth is meant to teach us how to view ourselves. Legend is oftentimes only storytelling. Myth is a psychological counseling session. Great empires – Greece, Rome, China, Japan, Sweden, Germany, and Britain, among others – have been built upon the mythology of the founding tribe of that empire. *The Faerie Queen* and *Beowulf* are still required reading in high-school classes the world over. This strong sense of the founding mythology has remained present, unfortunately often for evil purpose, throughout the centuries of these countries' existence. Nordic and Germanic mythology has plagued humankind for millennia. It was no coincidence that the violence-filled Germanic mythology fueled the rise of Nazism and helped cause a world war that consumed over forty million lives.

The Torah does not deal with myth per se. Yet the Flood and Noah's ark, the Tower of Babel, the centrality of the land of Israel, factual as they all are in the biblical narrative, nevertheless were all combined to create a basis for the holy mythology of the Jewish people. In addition, the idea that the "events of the works and decisions of our founders, the fathers of Israel, are a sure guidepost for their descendants" helped strengthen a mythology that binds the Jewish generations together and gives us insights into the values of Judaism and historical events, past and present. Part of that positive mythology is that the previous generations, especially those of biblical and Talmudic times, were of such great spiritual stature that we find it well-nigh impossible to comprehend them. The Talmud states, "If the previous generations were considered as angels then we can deem ourselves to be human beings. But if they were merely humans then we are as donkeys and not even equal to the donkey of Pineḥas ben Ya'ir [whose donkey was somehow able to discern permitted food from the forbidden]." This is a governing concept in Judaism, one that stands staunchly opposed to the modern tendency to delegitimize all past heroes and saints, and looks upon modern man as the equal if not greater than all that came before him. Many of the struggles and controversies in Jewish history revolve about this important issue. It remains a constant pattern in the story of the people of Israel. It is one of the major fault lines that today separate traditional Jewry from other Jews who deny that holy Jewish mythology and world view.

There are many types of fantasies that exist in Jewish life. There is a natural tendency among all humans to be nostalgic about the past – "the good old days." The truth of the matter is that "the good old days" may have been old but they rarely were good. Yet, this fantasy is still today a major one in the Jewish world, especially in the religiously observant Jewish society. The portrait of Jewish life that emerges from this oft repeated and taught fantasy is that Jewish life in eastern Europe, difficult as the physical conditions might have been, was spiritually wonderful and that Jews were somehow serene and happy in that time and place. Also part of the fantasy is that in eastern Europe Torah study was rampant, the Torah scholar was honored and treasured by the community and that almost everyone was observant of Jewish law and halakhic ritual. Books like A.J. Heschel's *The Earth Is the Lord's*, beautiful and emotionally comforting as the book is, contribute to this fantasy. This fantasy is not only false, it is terribly dangerous. It allows us to currently repeat the errors of the past that led to the secularization of the majority of the Jewish people in eastern Europe and to the breakdown of rabbinic and Torah authority. In the nineteenth century, Jews in eastern Europe became assimilated. They became Marxists and revolutionaries, secular and agnostic if not even atheistic. By the 1930s, seventy percent of all Jewish children in Poland no longer attended Jewish schools of any kind. Urbanization took a tremendous toll on traditional Jewish lifestyle. Terrible working conditions and onerous work hours in the city's factories destroyed the Sabbath for many. Child labor was common and unemployment in Jewish society reached astronomical figures. Poverty, disease and malnutrition were the lot of most of the Jewish masses. The educational system, the traditional *ḥeder*, the one-size-fits-all approach to curriculum and the students, all began to collapse of its own weight. The breakdown of the traditional Jewish world in the twentieth century, of which the Holocaust was naturally a very strong and dominant contributing factor, nevertheless began in nineteenth-century eastern Europe. It was not a phenomenon caused by America or modern Israel, though that is where the results of this breakdown of Jewish life are currently playing out. And, therefore, portraying and perpetuating the fantasy of eastern European Jewish life as idyllic is counterproductive to any attempts to build Torah Judaism today in America and Israel.

Other fantasies exist in the Jewish world. Superstitions abound. There are many charlatans in the Jewish world that prey on innocent people. Selling fantasies is big business, and it is thriving. Sexual abusers that hide behind religion and spirituality and mysterious fantasies of cures and raising the soul and other such nonsense in order to ply their sick schemes, are the stuff of often recurring scandals in our society. The fantasy that such pressing and dangerous problems as sexual deviancy, monetary cheating, criminal behavior, substance abuse, etc., cannot and do not exist in observant Jewish society is perpetuated, all real evidence to the contrary notwithstanding. People always prefer to whistle past the graveyard, and therefore this fantasy of perfection in our society persists. There is a fantasy that allegedly kabbalism-based healing exists and that therefore one should always pursue this type of alternative medicine. Prayer to God certainly helps and works but magical potions of holy water and other such fantasies are the stuff of the gullible and credulous, sold by the exploiters of other people's troubles, usually for personal monetary gain. Judaism is a very sophisticated faith. It does not lend itself to fantasies about things that are not real or beneficial. Yet superstitions exist because life itself is irrational and humans find it difficult to deal with. Therefore, fantasies are always with us and part of our psychological makeup. Some are very dangerous as I have pointed out above. Others are relatively benign. The rabbis of the Talmud always sought to dampen Jewish fantasies, even about the messianic era. But the pattern of recurring fantasies in Jewish life always reemerges in every generation and society. It is part of human nature – it may even be a necessary part – and Jews are no exception to the governing rules of human nature.

Then there exists in Jewish society outright falsifications about the past and the present. I mentioned earlier in this chapter the present day falsification of the real situation of nineteenth- and twentieth-century eastern European Jewry. Stories and descriptions about people and events are made up of whole cloth. The ideas and philosophies of great people of the past are twisted to make them conform to modern political correctness in sections of Jewish society. Whole biographies and historic events are simply erased if they do not conform to the current view of how things should be in the imagined perfect world. Photographs are doctored, skullcaps are added or removed, unpleasant incidents are sanitized – all in the name of advancing the true faith as it is currently understood to be. It is unfair to morph, for example, Rabbi Samson Raphael Hirsch of Frankfurt am Main and his ideas of Jewish education and life into being identical to those of a Lithuanian yeshiva head in the 1800s. Nor should the great controversies of Jewish life simply be erased from our knowledge because they present difficult issues for us to consider. The great people of the past are great enough and sufficiently resilient to face the past truthfully and intelligently. They need no false embellishments. I am convinced that it is the present persistent sense of insecurity, personally and as a group, of much of religious Jewry today that drives most of these falsifications and distortions of the past. As such, these falsifications ironically lead to lessened faith instead of their alleged goal of strengthening belief within Jewish society.

The penchant for anecdotal stories over analytical insights drives many an author or speaker today to create utterly false stories about the subject at hand. I know of a number of biographies about great men of the previous generation that record incidents in their lives that the families of these great people insist never happened. Most of the time these falsifications are relatively benign but some of them are really sad and dangerous. Many times a story that is basically true about one individual is now being told and ascribed to an entirely different individual. This is a terrible disservice to both individuals involved. There is a thin line separating legend from falsification. Falsification insists on being taken as fact and truth. It rewrites history to conform to its idea of right and wrong, good and bad, fair and unfair. It purposely intends to mislead, and advance an agenda of its own. It is this tendency that makes falsification so dangerous for, by perverting history and biography, it robs us of the ability to truly learn valuable lessons from the past and from the great people who lived then. Truth has to win out eventually; it will always find its way, and the more falsifications piled on it only makes its eventual emergence more shocking and traumatic. All authors and historians indulge in some sort of poetic license in their works. But crossing the line into outright falsification is a wrong that should not be easily tolerated by the Jewish world.

So again, separating the wheat from the chaff of Jewish history and biography has been an ongoing pattern throughout Jewish history. We find it in the Talmud and in all later works of Jewish scholarship. Since we can assume that the falsifiers amongst us will always be present in every generation, the task of searching for the truth of our past will also always be with us. Just as the scholars of Israel throughout the ages have labored mightily to present us with a correct text of our holy books, free of emendations and copyist errors, so, too, there should continue to be an effort to present us with a record of Jewish history and biography free from purposeful or negligent falsifications. We have a great deal to learn from the past. One of those lessons is that a false history is as dangerous as, if not more dangerous than, no history at all.

Afterword

I was very challenged in writing this book. Although much of it is factually based, it is really a record of my opinions on many current issues in Jewish life. I have formed my opinions by reviewing the history of the Jewish people and focusing on the recurring patterns of that amazing and almost unbelievable story. The topics covered in this book are as fresh today as they were millennia ago. But every generation, while facing apparently the same challenges and problems of the past, has of necessity a unique view and method in dealing with those problems and challenges. Thus, approaches and policies that may have succeeded in past centuries are perhaps no longer relevant to dealing with the very same issues a few generations later. Circumstances and influences change. A great Torah sage once remarked that the generations of the Jewish people are to be compared to individual ships that must traverse a great ocean of water. Although many ships have previously crossed this body of water, every ship nevertheless has to find its own way across it anew. Yet the navigational skills of the previous ships are of aid and instruction to the latter ships. This book attempted to show how the Jewish people, in dealing with great and dangerous issues that constantly confronted it, were able to traverse the sea of its history. Not all of our ships made it across the sea of history. But the main flagship of Israel is still sailing confidently, no matter how rough the seas.

In writing this book I was forced to think about many of the issues that comprise this work. If this book has any purpose for the reader it is exactly that – to make one think about issues that confront the Jewish and general world and not be satisfied with flippant, quick and pat answers to those problems and issues. The pressures of everyday life, the torrent of media information thrust upon us daily and hourly, and the personal difficulties that all of us face in living and coping, oftentimes do not allow us the time or energy to think about deep issues and overriding values of life. The trees obscure the forest. I learned a great deal about the Jewish people and about myself as a Jew and as a person in writing this book. A great man once said that it is worthwhile for a scholar to travel half the world in order to stand before ten Jews and deliver a five-minute-long insight in Torah before the commencement of the evening prayer service, so that they may now pray with better intensity, even if the only one affected by the Torah lesson is the speaker himself! Every author writes for himself, and every public speaker really speaks to himself. Nevertheless, there are many who can benefit from the introspection of an author or public speaker. I can only hope that this be the case here too.

About the Author

Rabbi Berel Wein is a scholar, lecturer, writer and leading expert on Jewish history. For more than twenty-five years, he has worked to popularize Jewish history through lectures, films, seminars, television and radio appearances and educational tours. He is the founder and director of the Destiny Foundation, an educational media organization that produces multi-media Jewish history programs.

Rabbi Wein is a graduate of the Hebrew Theological College and Roosevelt College in Chicago. He received his Juris Doctor from De Paul University Law School, and a Doctor of Hebrew Letters from Hebrew Theological College. From 1964 until 1972, he served as Rabbi of the Beth Israel Congregation in Miami Beach, Florida. For the following twenty-four years, he was Rabbi of Congregation Bais Torah in Suffern, New York. In 1977, he founded Yeshiva Shaarei Torah in Suffern and served as its *Rosh Yeshiva* until 1997. Rabbi Wein also was executive vice president of the Union of Orthodox Organizations of America, and served for five years as the rabbinic administrator of its Kashrut Division.

Rabbi Wein is the recipient of the Educator of the Year Award from the Covenant Foundation, and the Torah Educators Prize from Makhon HaRav Frank in Jerusalem. He is a regular columnist for *The*

Jerusalem Post, and the author of many books, including *Vision & Valor: An Illustrated History of the Talmud,* also available from Maggid Books. He lives in Jerusalem.

The fonts used in this book are from the Arno family

Other works by Berel Wein
available from Maggid

Vision and Valor: An Illustrated History of the Talmud

Maggid Books
The best of contemporary Jewish thought from
Koren Publishers Jerusalem